WORDSWORTH
AND THE VOCABULARY
OF EMOTION

WORDSWORTH
AND THE VOCABULARY
OF EMOTION

BY

JOSEPHINE MILES

1 9 6 5
OCTAGON BOOKS, INC.
NEW YORK

Reprinted 1965
by special arrangement with University of California Press

OCTAGON BOOKS, INC.
175 FIFTH AVENUE
NEW YORK, N. Y. 10010

LIBRARY OF CONGRESS CATALOG CARD NUMBER: 65-16785

Printed in U.S.A. by
NOBLE OFFSET PRINTERS, INC.
NEW YORK 3, N. Y.

To J. L. M.
FROM Z TO A

ACKNOWLEDGMENT

A GREAT DEBT of mine is to Professor Benjamin H. Lehman, to Professors James R. Caldwell, Bertrand H. Bronson, George R. Potter, and the Department of English itself, for aid, argument, and generosity.

J. M.

PREFACE TO THE OCTAGON EDITION

In the quarter-century since this study of Wordsworth's explicitness was made, explicitness of feeling in poetry has taken on new virtues—the virtues of directness, forthrightness, simple communicativeness, as distinct from the obliquities of association which earlier seemed to poets so valuable. With the work of Robert Lowell, W. D. Snodgrass, Anne Sexton, Denise Levertov, we learn again, though in worlds of thought far from Wordsworth, how potently feelings can be felt and formulated.

Perhaps therefore some longer view of the changing relations of emotions to objects or states of experience may be relevant to a present reading of this book, and, in turn, this book relevant to processes of literal experience as our poetry perceives them.

As my more recent studies in *Eras and Modes in English Poetry* have shown, and as I hope to suggest further in work on prose style, the concern with literal meaning of feeling, the naming of essential responses, has never been absent from English poetry. Rather it has faded during some times and prospered during others. The name of *love,* the noun and verb of *love,* has persisted throughout, but most other terms, except *heart,* love's location, have come and gone. Until the Renaissance, emotional words were partly evaluative, as in *fair, dear, sweet,* or social, as in *noble* and *gentle,* or of spiritual relation, as in *mercy* and *grace, faith* and *glory,* if one would call these at least partly emotional.

With Wyatt in mid-sixteenth century the new poetry of complaint began for England, carrying on the *pain* of James I of Scotland in *cruel, desire, tear, woe, please,* and the metaphor of feeling, *fire,* to which Surrey added *flame.* Then the poets of the golden era tempered their *grief* with *hope,* their *proud* and *happy* with *sad,* in classical and pastoral balance. And after them, in the seventeenth century came the innovations of exuberence, divine enthusiasm: such terms in dominant use as Campion's *joy,* Herbert's *praise,* More's *sense,* Roscommon's partly emotional *wild,* Walsh's *charm,* Pomfret's *delight.* All of these terms were used widely also by their fellow poets. Where Wyatt and Surrey had each stressed perhaps a dozen terms of emotion, mainly woeful, and a half-century later, Daniel and Campion had played the full Elizabethan melody of half-again as many, no one until the century after, not even Crashaw with his *weeping,* not even Roscommon with intensive *sense,* achieved the varied emotional expression of Walsh's and Pomfret's neoclassical literalness, their *charming, fair, happy, fear, breast, heart, joy, love, pain, passion, pity, tear, torment, hate, love,* their *gay, sad, delight,* and *cry.*

Another century later, it was Crabbe who turned emotion into new explicitness by stressing again its more sombre variety, in *fair, happy, humble, proud, sad, care, fear, grief, hope, joy, pain, pleasure, pride, woe, to feel.* He began a new sway of emotional explication—for Burns, for Bowles, for Wordsworth, for Southey, for Moore, and Keats—and this, while not quite as strong as in Pomfret's time, is yet rich, in addition to that time's characteristic *happy, sad, joy, love, pain, passion,* with *mournful, weary, fancy, pity, sorrow, woe, feeling,* and *weeping.* Wordsworth's *dear, sweet, joy, pain, loving* and *weeping,* and Keats' *happy, sad, sweet, joy, love, pain, pleasure, sorrow, woe* thus make a blend of earlier enthusiams and later moderations. Crabbe's characteristic early use of *pleasure* and *to feel*, Blake's *to weep*, Bowles' *sorrow*, these, along with Rogers' *memory* and Moore's *dream*, are the last innovations for major terms of explicitly named emotion in English poetry. After them the tide of natural forces, first appearing hesitantly with Sylvester's *sea* and Milton's *wind*, Vaughan's *cloud* and Blackmore's *land*, Thomson's *mountain* and Warton's *field*, suddenly in the later eighteenth century strengthens and fills, with Bowles' *wave* and *wood*, Wordsworth's *tree*, Coleridge's phenomenal *bird, body, moon, water*, Moore's *star*, Keats' *wing*, and then all the recent terminology of *rain, grass, hill, snow, leaf*, and *stone*, which ends in Auden's *nothing*. Not only in invention but in amount, emotion is subordinate to natural force, so that we see in highly emotional poets like Swinburne or Yeats only two or three recurrent terms of *sad* or *sweet, love* or *sorrow*.

Our era then is like mid-sixteenth, mid-seventeenth, or mid-eighteenth centuries, when Scots moralities, or metaphysical metaphors and concepts, or neoclassical scenes and generalities provided modes of feeling other than literal naming. Our future, like theirs, may well be coming around, as we see it in the newest poetry, to passion again.

Those who in the past decade have written of Wordsworth's poetry have emphasized its quality of process, the on-going of experience which we are drawn to share. What I would emphasize about this sharing of process is that it is a sharing also of interpretation of process; that is, that the poet not only undergoes, but remembers the undergoing, and in tranquillity decides and tells what it has meant to him in terms of joy or sorrow, hope or fear. Therefore the poetic texture is not presentative but interpretive, not implicative and evocative but declarative in its relation to human feeling. Emotion is not only the occasion of poetic statement by Wordsworth, but its predicate.

JOSEPHINE MILES
December 1964

CONTENTS

I. THE NAMING OF EMOTION

THE PROBLEM

To WRITE at length and with some pleasure of Wordsworth's vocabulary of stated emotion is not willfully to ignore present taste and present critical theory. Grant that *leaves laughing in glee* and *men made happy by the scene* do not seem now especially poetic; grant that not only George Moore, Hulme, Eastman, but more recently Eliot, Richards, Tate, Ransom, Brooks, and the poetry-vs.-science theorists, have placed either Wordsworth or named emotion outside and away from "pure poetry" and "the tradition," still Wordsworth's persistent and formal naming of emotion, having been attentively heard as poetry once, and possibly to be heard so again, may be closely observed now to some good end.

The end I have in mind is different from that of contemporary critics. They are working to establish, by revaluations of the past, a pattern fit for, and characteristic of, the present. They are making clear the needs, tastes, standards, values, effective works of today, and then they are looking at the past in the light of these, so that past, present, and possible future in our minds may be a working whole with some stability and coherence. Consequently these modern critics strengthen and freshen the modern world of poetry; they cast off many trailing lines of nineteenth-century interpretation (still present for textbooks and learners from them), and they relegate from focus to fringe much of the world of poetry that seems not now important because not now essentially poetic.

While "essentiallly poetic" is a phrase the value of which is denied by many of these critics, as it is used by their predecessors, it is a phrase they use by implication themselves, and it is a phrase that I use in explication without any disapprobation at all, but with a sense of the limits of time in it. This perhaps is a difference between critical and historical study: that the critical takes for light on its material, whatever that material may be, the illumination provided by the values of the critics' own day; whereas the historical, though still limited in its interests by its own time, looks for lights in focus as from the time of the material it is attempting to observe.

Thus, "essentially poetic" means for 1940, say, a certain vigorous consensus in poetic practice and opinion in 1940 and the years it takes to be its period. "Essentially" in these terms means the best, the most central, as closely as it can now be construed. We arrange the pattern of poetic history in these terms. Some poetry is more, some poetry is less, poetic to us. Wordsworth's, with its statement of emotion called "prosaic," is evidently less.[1]

But, on the other hand, having achieved some self-assurance from recognition of a present pattern as expertly formulated as ours has recently been, one may recognize the integrity of patterns other than this one, and have some curiosity about the details of their formation. My purpose, then, is rather the description of some poetry than prescription for it, and the means to that end must necessarily be observation as detailed, enumeration as careful, separation of units as distinct, though as provisional, as

---

[1] For critical contrasts of poetic language and prosaic language see: John Livingston Lowes, *Convention and Revolt in Poetry,* p. 8; Max Eastman, *The Literary Mind,* p. 84; C. K. Ogden and I. A. Richards, *The Meaning of Meaning,* p. 271; F. W. Bateson, *English Poetry and the English Language,* p. 17; H. F. Sampson, *The Language of Poetry,* p. 23; A. E. Housman, *The Name and Nature of Poetry,* p. 45.

See also: Paul Valéry's "Concerning 'The Cimetière Marin,'" *Southern Review* (summer, 1938); and John Crowe Ransom's basic opposition of aesthetic to efficient, imaginatively particular to scientifically universal, and knowledge to use, and his dislike of "Platonic poetry," in *The World's Body,* as on pp. x, 31, 45, 120, 130, 216, etc. Allen Tate is distinguished among current critics for placing such opposition within poetry. See "Tension in Poetry," *Southern Review* (summer, 1938).

See also: Herbert Read, *Form in Modern Poetry,* p. 39; J. G. Jennings, *Metaphor in Poetry,* p. 37; Allen Tate, *Reactionary Essays on Poetry and Ideas,* p. 112; William Empson, *Seven Kinds of Ambiguity,* p. 319; Ogden and Richards, *The Meaning of Meaning,* p. 272. Although it may be suggested that such divisions are in *functions* of language, and not in specific kinds of words, one has only to note Richards' wariness of the actual words of emotion, and Eastman's analysis of why *ruddy* is more poetic than *red* (*op. cit.,* p. 174), to see that the distinctions are not limited to function in practice. Empson, *Some Versions of Pastoral,* p. 125: "Happiness ... as a rule it is a weak word."

possible. My use for "essentially" aims to be Wordsworth's use, even though no more than a mild approximation may be possible. Every poem and, more generally, every period of poetry has an "essentially" of its own; Wordsworth's own is not ours, but it has a continuous importance as it is part of the sum of possible poetic essentials.

Though strictly set off in the academic historical field of attempted description, a study of Wordsworth's vocabulary of emotion may yet be suspected of liability in this way: too many scholars have already intended to describe things *as they are*—Dryden "the man," the "real sources" of *Paradise Lost,* Ruskin's "attitude toward art"—only to find that all these are seen to be something else a few years later. No numbers of footnotes seem to add up to an incorruptible objectivity.

For example, what is Wordsworth's poetry about? In what is it like poetry of the century before it and poetry of the century after? What relation does it have to Wordsworth's theories of poetry and poetic diction? These questions have been answered not once but several hundred times, with a degree of variation vast enough to trouble the toughest scholar into a further attempt to clear the field and answer each one finally. Have, then, the studies of Wordsworth by Harper, Legouis, Garrod, Read, Rice, Raleigh, Beatty, Banerjee, Barstow, and of his times by Dobrée, Beach, Cobban, Campbell, Elton, Herford, Lucas been descriptive to a useful degree of recurrence and agreement? In large part they have, and they become increasingly so as skill in the technique increases. Many recent dissertations seem to me as exciting reading in the realm of fact as one could find. But where they depart from their province, they do so, I think, for two reasons.

First, and more commonly in the past than now, they do so because they assume just one real and essential period, poet, and poem, and take no protection against a storm of other possibilities.

Thus many have done with Wordsworth, naming as his major characteristics those rare qualities which they found praiseworthy in him, being in this measure critics, not observers. And second, they depart from their province because the observers observe a field so wide that they are forced constantly to make selections within it, these selections being based not on their materials' emphasis, but on their own. As a result, the final picture, as they purportedly describe it, is a picture they themselves have just got through trimming.

Here is why I feel a lack in this imprecision: it was my own difficulty as I began studying Wordsworth. Reading the *Lyrical Ballads* and the *Prelude,* I was oppressed by a constant insistence on what seemed to be considered the stuff of life in just so many words—hope, joy, fears, tears, laughter, moods, affections, passions, and all the other labeled responses in terms of names of emotions. I felt that, so exposed, it was poor stuff and poor poetry. Yet, because of the magnitude and popularity of Wordsworth, I had no wish but to assume he was something of a poet and knew what he was about. Seeing already why my contemporaries pitied his plight of time, place, disposition, and taste, by virtue of his flat, obvious, prosaic, literal statement of feeling, I needed plain facts about his intentions and his ideas of poetic language, through which to discover whether Wordsworth had any notion of the unpoetic character of this evidently beloved material. Wordsworth scholarship, large though it is, did not supply any nearly complete answer to what seems to me a fundamental and even naïve question. Why it did not was, as I have suggested, that it was prescriptive, evaluating the stated feeling as either finely perceived or deeply mistaken; or because it was selective, choosing to concern itself with some terms only, without an expressed pattern of selection. So even the books which have inquired most specifically into Wordsworth's theories of poetic diction presented divergent answers: his discussion was all in terms of *meta-*

phor, or of *word order,* or of *general vocabulary.* One could only ask finally, which? Dazzling concrete detail represented the real Wordsworth, or elegant abstract statement, or rural simplicity. But which? And why did he so devote himself to the vocabulary of *love, hate, fear;* was this a part of his "real language of men"?

Hence the necessity that I answer my own question about Wordsworth's vocabulary, and that I establish the premise that an answer is possible in relatively objective terms. If both critics and academicians tend to summon up personal and local values when they use the word *poetic,* is it after all possible for anyone to inquire with any degree of accuracy what was *poetic* for Wordsworth? I do think some quantitative measures are available.

In baldest form, I think one may count certain words or types of words in a poet's work, to discover predominances. One may observe the contexts of these words to find recurring types of connection and alliance. Words and contexts most used by a poet or a period of poetry are apt to name just those combinations and relations of things which are important to that poet and time, and which are therefore worth the trouble, dignity, and force, all the special qualities, of a poetic form. If, then, one notices, even is oppressed by, the sound of *I feared, I was happy,* in the *Lyrical Ballads* and the *Prelude,* the first question is whether their amount is as great, whether their recurrence is as persistent, as it seems. The best way to find out is to count. Otherwise, the abundance might have its being in the sensitivity of the reader rather than in the stress of the writer. The steps of inquiry, then, take place as follows:

1) Establishment of the words to be included in the limits of "vocabulary of emotion," the names of emotion and standard signs of emotion.

2) Counting of the number of names (also called statements, limited to single words) in every poem, group, and in the com-

plete poetical works of Wordsworth, in terms of occurrence of such names by number of lines.

3) Observation and classification of main kinds of immediate context: that is to say, with respect to those things with which the named emotions are most closely connected in phrases in which they appear.

4) Relation of the body of this vocabulary and context (*a*) to the author's poetry as a whole, (*b*) to his critical thinking and philosophical view, particularly as expressed in his prose, and (*c*) to the same vocabulary as used by other poets in the same and other periods.

There is still plenty of room in this procedure for the writer to insert his own interpretations; but the reader has at every moment of the study a knowledge of just how much statement is verifiable and of how much is surmise.[2]

Consider what traditional problems could be moved a little toward solution by the sort of knowledge a great many detailed

[2] One is supported in such method by the generalizations of the younger critics: by Blackmur's that the meaning of a poem, the part of it that is intellectually formulable, must depend upon "the facts about the meanings of the elements aside from their final meaning in combination"; and by Empson's "Now, evidently the appreciator has got to be an analyst, because the only way to say a complicated thing more simply is to separate it into its parts and say each of them in turn. . . . One cannot conceive observation except in terms of comparison, or comparison except as based on recognition." And note Valéry's appreciation of scholarly attention to "those recurrences of terms that reveal the bent, the characteristic frequencies of a mind."

See R. P. Blackmur, *The Double Agent*, p. 298; Empson, *Seven Types of Ambiguity*, pp. 316, 319; Valéry, "Concerning '*The Cimetière Marin.*'" M. Valéry adds the parenthesis: "Certain words keep ringing in us more than any others, like overtones of our profoundest nature . . ."

The necessity for distinguishing between immediate and historical, or evaluative and accumulative, meanings, has been illustrated by Kenneth Burke in *Counter-statement*, p. 251: "Since certain things were believed, and poets used these beliefs to produce poetic effects, the beliefs became 'poetic.' But in the course of time contrary things came to be believed, with the consequence that the earlier beliefs were now called 'illusions.' And noting that so much of the world's poetry had been built upon what were now called illusions, the critics argued in a circle: The illusions, they said, were poetic, and in the loss of illusions through science we face the death of poetry through science. The difficulty lay in the assumption that illusions were inherently 'poetic'—whereas they had been made 'poetic' by the fact that poets had constructed poetry upon them."

Two books which make larger contributions toward the solving of these problems than many heretofore, but too recently for discussion in this study, are Raymond D. Havens' *The Mind of a Poet* (Johns Hopkins Press, 1942) and Frederick A. Pottle's *The Idiom of Poetry* (Cornell Univ. Press, 1941).

studies of poetic vocabulary could provide. What words by stress—emphasis of elaboration and repetition and abundance in many poets—have been most important to poetry? Have their references and their contexts altered widely? By the words that poetry chooses, is it possible to know as important the things, qualities, actions that poets and their times have considered important? How do new words enter the realm of poetic publicity and grow in favor and become prime? What, in other words, are some of the relations of the language of poetry to language in general, not only in respect to *ordonnance,* as Coleridge would have it, but in respect to simple presence of terms?

A few studies of such problems have been made in the past two decades. The fashion and interest which have brought I. A. Richards' *The Meaning of Meaning,* Stuart Chase's popular *The Tyranny of Words,* and many others, have brought increased work of the type of Barfield's *Poetic Diction,* Bateson's historical study, Lowes', Empson's, Spurgeon's on Shakespeare's images, and R. P. Blackmur's "close criticism." Most of these, however, are more general than the study here proposed will have to be.

"Wordsworth and the Vocabulary of Emotion," then, has not much assistance from tradition, and is the worse for that. But it participates in raising all the general questions which any study of poetic vocabulary, as I have suggested, must raise; and it further raises and perhaps answers some of the traditional questions involved in discussions of Wordsworth and the Romantics. Was stated emotion characteristic of romantic as opposed to or in agreement with neoclassic poetry? What place did it have in Wordsworth's criticism of his predecessors, in his revolutionary moves in poetry, in his philosophy of "real" language? Did his theory and his practice agree in regard to it, and was his audience pleased by the result in its terms? What did these words have to say that the worlds of Johnson and of Arnold were equally ready to hear?

In one sense, when we know so little about what poets have had to say, when we can scarcely tell that *cloud* has been important to one age and not to another, and in what special way; and how *bone* and *leaf* as words now wield a power in poetry they never had before; when we are in this state of curiosity, almost any place in poetry is a good place to begin looking around. It is perhaps true, however, that 1800 is a particularly suitable place. Wordsworth brought the poetic-diction argument into the open, and that field of argument has grown no grass as yet; the debate is still lively. The time and Wordsworth have had some credit for establishing the character of modern poetry; can that be allowed them in the special terms of stated emotion? The era is far enough away to look at, and not so far as to be quaint. Coleridge has still his force for interpretation in what people say of poetry and of the *Lyrical Ballads* and the *Prelude* today; and people still talk of these books as if they were alive. But above all, Wordsworth's consciousness of his purpose, and his iron consistency in establishing, restating, and poetizing upon it, give us good ground for observation of the life of words in a poet's mind.

THE MATERIAL

This is "Lines Written in Early Spring," a poem by William Wordsworth in the first volume of the *Lyrical Ballads,* 1798:

> I heard a thousand blended notes,
> While in a grove I sate reclined,
> In that sweet mood when pleasant thoughts
> Bring sad thoughts to the mind.
>
> To her fair works did Nature link
> The human soul that through me ran;
> And much it grieved my heart to think
> What man has made of man.
>
> Through primrose tufts, in that green bower,
> The periwinkle trailed its wreaths;
> And 'tis my faith that every flower
> Enjoys the air it breathes.

The birds around me hopped and played,
Their thoughts I cannot measure:
But the least motion which they made
It seemed a thrill of pleasure.

The budding twigs spread out their fan,
To catch the breezy air;
And I must think, do all I can,
That there was pleasure there.

If this belief from heaven be sent,
If such be Nature's holy plan,
Have I not reason to lament
What man has made of man?

Though Wordsworth sat reclined in this grove and watched these birds and felt these feelings, he was under no compulsion of nature or art to made his poem about them in just such one-two-three fashion, or in fact to make any poem at all of the material. No doubt we have in English poetry many poems inspired or composed in just such circumstances: they may have ignored the specific scene, or they may have used it as "objective correlative" for entirely another mood, or they may have concentrated on its sensed qualities to the exclusion of statements about the emotions aroused and attributed. From some poets one should expect no notice of primrose tufts or periwinkle at all; from most modern poets one would be sure of more color, texture, pattern, and sensed fact about these plants. Where is the poetry in the event?

For Wordsworth it was clearly not in color and texture. Details of these he had perceived and noted well enough to remember for a half century,[3] but he gave them no place in the poem. The prose note to the poem reads:

Actually composed while I was sitting by the side of the brook that runs down from the Comb, in which stands the village of Alford,

---

[3] In 1843 he dictated some of his poem notes to Miss Fenwick, and later wrote more for the 1849–50 edition. See, for all, the edition by E. Dowden (London, 1892), esp. Pref., p. 12.

through the grounds of Alfoxden. It was a chosen resort of mine. The brook fell down a sloping rock so as to make a waterfall considerable for that country, and across the pool below had fallen a tree, an ash if I rightly remember, from which rose perpendicularly, boughs in search of the light intercepted by the deep shade above. The boughs bore leaves of green that for want of sunshine had faded into almost lily-white; and from the underside of this natural sylvan bridge depended long and beautiful tresses of ivy which waved gently in the breeze that might poetically speaking be called the breath of the waterfall.

For many modern readers the rhythm of the first sentence, the boughs in search of the light, the color of leaves are the poetry. But for Wordsworth these were the material of a prose note. For moderns the regular object-to-response-and-back-again pattern of the "Lines" is prosáic, the birds' thrill of pleasure and the reason to lament are prosaic; but for Wordsworth they were worth the pattern and dignity of "Lines," they were poetic.

It may be said that this is a very simple poem, even a poor poem. It is at one end of the scale that critics tend to draw in the *Lyrical Ballads,* with "Tintern Abbey" at the other end. "Tintern Abbey" is, in its persistent statement of emotion, however, just like the "Lines in Early Spring." It begins with a fact and a sound.

> Five years have past; five summers, with the length
> Of five long winters! and again I hear
> These waters, rolling from their mountain-springs
> With a soft inland murmur.

And it proceeds from these, the lofty cliffs, the plot of cottage-ground, the wreaths of smoke, directly to prolonged explicit statement of the "blessed mood."

> These beauteous forms,
> Through a long absence, have not been to me
> As is a landscape to a blind man's eye:
> But oft, in lonely rooms, and 'mid the din
> Of towns and cities, I have owed to them
> In hours of weariness, sensations sweet,
> Felt in the blood, and felt along the heart;
> And passing even into my purer mind,

> With tranquil restoration:—feelings too
> Of unremembered pleasure: such, perhaps,
> As have no slight or trivial influence
> On that best portion of a good man's life,
> His little, nameless, unremembered, acts
> Of kindness and of love.

Here is a new distinction, a loving care and sense of expert detail given to the phrasing of the sensations sweet and the feelings of unremembered pleasure—a kind of tentative exactitude which subordinates all else the poem may have to say to this particular weighing of emotional value.

As the poem looks to past, to present, to future, it names and considers this value again and again, establishing after each experience its consequent emotional effect. It persists in the statement of "aching joys" and "dizzy raptures," of "wild ecstacies" and "sober pleasure," of "fear, or pain, or grief," and "tender joy." It is evident that an increase of skill for Wordsworth, a new assurance in treating of word and line, brought pleasure in ability to move the substance of stated feeling to further degrees of discrimination. The scene of "Tintern Abbey," like the scene of the "Lines," was poetic to Wordsworth only so far as it justly gave rise to feeling; further precise details would be finicking. The close bond between sense and emotion, between natural object and human response, he stated metaphorically in the lines

> The sounding cataract
> Haunted me like a passion: the tall rock,
> The mountain, and the deep and gloomy wood,
> Their colors and their forms, were then to me
> An appetite; a feeling and a love,
> That had no need of a remoter charm,
> By thought supplied, nor any interest
> Unborrowed from the eye.

Here is an identification which finds for objects a function different from that which we may now see in them, a different set of connections in poetry from that which we tend to make.

The lyrical "Lines" and the meditative "Tintern Abbey" are two varieties of poem from the *Lyrical Ballads;* the third is narrative, the closest to the "ballad" title. To see that Wordsworth uses his fact-to-feeler-to-feeling consistently in all types, one may look to the narratives, to "The Idiot Boy," which most critics have disliked, which Wordsworth wrote "almost extempore—never wrote anything with so much glee."[4] It is a narrative, and thus has opportunity for suggestion and implication of mood by action and atmosphere. Unlike "Lines in Early Spring," it is not personal and calls for no audible philosophical reaction by emotion. Nevertheless it does not spare the statement of emotion; not author's here, but actors'. Atmosphere is not enough for the poem. Says the note, " 'The Cocks did crow to-whoo, to-whoo, And the sun did shine so cold'—is the foundation of the whole," and the first stanza begins in that tone:

> 'Tis eight o'clock,—a clear March night,
> The moon is up,—the sky is blue,
> The owlet, in the moonlight air,
> Shouts from nobody knows where;
> He lengthens out his lonely shout,
> Halloo! halloo! a long halloo!

But if that is the foundation it is not the main structure, and the second stanza is of different stuff:

> —Why bustle thus about your door,
> What means this bustle, Betty Foy?
> Why are you in this mighty fret,
> And why on horseback have you set
> Him whom you love, your Idiot Boy?

The distorted world, we see, is not going to be used to suggest the minds and hearts perceiving it, by its own distortion, but is to be accompanied, pace for pace, by terms which name the emotional situation directly. "Him whom you love, your Idiot Boy," is with variations to be the refrain line, and just as the word *idiot* will

---

[4] Fenwick note to "The Idiot Boy."

appear through all the variations, so will the word *love,* because
we must have more than an indicated state of mind, we must have
an explicit state of passion.

The stress is on the mother's passion, but the idiot and the pony,
too, participate in familiar emotions. Johnny's lips more than once
burr with joy:

> For joy he cannot hold the bridle,
> For joy his head and heels are idle,
> He's idle all for very joy.

And as for the pony, he is mild and good, "Whether he be in
joy or pain." Evenly along the course of the plot the vocabulary
makes plain the feeling, simply, in lines like "Oh! happy, happy,
happy John," "Poor Betty, in this sad distemper," "O woe is me!
O woe is me!" "These fears can never be endured," "Oh me! it is
a merry meeting"; with more vivid and adventurous figures as,
"Stands fixed, her face with joy o'erflows," "And Betty's drooping
at the heart," "And almost stifled with her bliss."

Wordsworth made two precise and therefore notable remarks
about this poem: one, that "the cocks did crow to-whoo, to-whoo,
and the sun did shine so cold" is the foundation of the whole; the
other, that the poem traces "the maternal passion through many
of its more subtle windings."[5] Both in immediate reference and
in wider atmosphere these statements are so far apart that one
would expect two separate poems from them; the language itself
suggests two distinct ways of thought; yet for Wordsworth they
are not only compatible, but poetic material in combination. So
in "The Idiot Boy" with its intense and purposeful inconsequence,
just as before in the "Lines Written in Early Spring" with its
meditative musing, the objects of sight and hearing and the abstract names of states of mind substantially accompany each other.

These "subtle windings of the maternal passion": they have
names like love and joy, as we have seen. They seem today to us,

---

[5] Fenwick note and Preface, 1802, respectively.

however, subtler and more effective when they rise out of an indirect observation:

> So, through the moonlight lane she goes,
> And far into the moonlight dale;
> And how she ran, and how she walked,
> And all that to herself she talked,
> Would surely be a tedious tale.
>
> In high and low, above, below,
> In great and small, in round and square,
> In tree and tower was Johnny seen,
> In bush and brake, in black and green;
> 'Twas Johnny, Johnny, everywhere.
>
> —She listens, but she cannot hear
> The foot of horse, the voice of man;
> The streams with softest sound are flowing,
> The grass you almost hear it growing,
> You hear it now, if e'er you can.

Through all the four hundred and fifty lines goes such phrasing, and in its sum I think it satisfying as the tracing of passion; but Wordsworth clearly did not think it so, for constantly, and especially in his climax, he has to say definitely:

> She looks again—her arms are up—
> She screams—she cannot move for joy;
> She darts, as with a torrent's force,
> She almost has o'erturned the horse,
> And fast she holds her Idiot Boy.
>
> And Johnny burrs, and laughs aloud;
> Whether in cunning or in joy
> I cannot tell; but while he laughs,
> Betty a drunken pleasure quaffs
> To hear again her Idiot Boy.
>
> —She kisses o'er and o'er again
> Him whom she loves, her Idiot Boy;
> She's happy here, is happy there,
> She is uneasy everywhere;
> Her limbs are all alive with joy.

It would be hard, if one were attending to the verse as it sounds, appears, and means in itself, not to be aware of an insistence upon a kind of language here: that which, with all its variety and shading, is concentrated upon calling emotions by their names and thus bodying them forth in words. In contrast to the sun and cocks of the poem, which by standing for other objects stand for a large field of faintly suggested emotions also, these words signify specific states. The contrast is not simply between abstract and concrete language, though that is part of it; the names for emotions are in a measure abstract, but it is evident already that Wordsworth's treatment of them in context is often concretely figurative and pictorial; further, there are countless other kinds of abstractions, plain and figured, besides the names for emotions. The contrast which these poems have by their very practice illustrated, and which might not even suggest itself in other poetry, is simply that between statement of emotion on the one hand and all the ways of implying it on the other.

One has surmised, reading the modern critics, that most of the ways of implying feeling now seem more effective than statement itself. I. A. Richards warns, " 'Putting it into words,' if the words are those of a psychological text book, is a process which may well be damaging to the feelings."[6] "There is a big difference between controlling and conveying feelings and talking about them."[7] Eliot advises, ". . . The only way of expressing emotion in the form of art is by finding an 'objective correlative'—such that when the external facts, which must terminate in sensory experience are given, the emotion is immediately evoked";[8] evoked by the object, not placed beside it. Blackmur praises Eliot for writing lines which suggest individual emotions without names.[9] Hulme calls it a defect of language that "it is only able to fix the objective and impersonal aspect of the emotions which we feel"—by nam-

---

[6] I. A. Richards, *Practical Criticism*, p. 186.   [7] Richards, *op. cit.*, App. A, p. 355.
[8] Quoted by F. O. Matthiessen, *Achievement of T. S. Eliot*, p. 57.
[9] Blackmur, "T. S. Eliot," *Hound and Horn*, I:3, 4.

ing them.[10] MacLeish suggests the use of objects to signify un-
stated feelings: "For all the history of grief, An empty doorway
and a maple leaf."[11]

With this background of prescription, certainly effective for our
own day, and with such various examples of poetically implied
feeling as Rossetti's "Honeysuckle," Eliot's "Death by Water,"
and the many poems of the Imagists in mind, one may well devote attention to details of the pattern of statement rising from
Wordsworth's quite different poetic policy. These, as we have
already noted, are classifications to be made in the pattern: first,
the words to be counted as names of emotion; second, the varieties
of their immediate contexts and the pattern of their use; third,
their number as by the line throughout Wordsworth's work. The
fourth group of questions, relating to their wider associations,
will be considered later.

First, as to the boundaries of the vocabulary of emotion, it sim-
plifies matters to include just those words which were considered
in Wordsworth's own day to be names of emotions. These were
the general terms such as *passion* and *affection;* the more specific,
such as *love, hate, fear;* and signs such as *tears, laughter,* and the
word *heart.* They ranged in Wordsworth's day a middle way
from sensations to concepts, leading from the simpler to the
more complex, from lower to higher—from sight of flower, by
feeling of joy, to crown of moral good, and so forth. Whatever the
distinctions made variously from Hobbes to Mill and from Johnson's Dictionary to the modern summaries of the New English
Dictionary, the main functions and examples have been constant,
and the agreement of terms general. *Passion, feeling, emotion*
have been used interchangeably; and *pleasure* near sensation,
faith near concept, both are included by convention. The New
English Dictionary quotes as the first definition of the passions

[10] T. E. Hulme, *Speculations,* ed. Herbert Read, p. 165.
[11] Archibald MacLeish, "Ars Poetica," *Collected Poems* (Boston, Houghton Mifflin,
1933).

that by Norris in 1710 (reflecting the new interest in them): "By the Passions I think we are to understand certain Motions of the Mind depending upon and accompanied with an Agitation of the Spirits." And the definition in the Defoe dictionary of 1735 is "affection, transport of mind; as Love, Hatred, etc."[12]

Three definitions of Wordsworth's time reveal the sense of definiteness the users of the terms seemed to have. The Encyclopedia Britannica in 1797: "The common division of the passions into *desire* and *aversion, hope* and *fear, joy* and *grief, love* and *hatred,* has been mentioned by every writer who has treated of them." Brown in 1810: "Consciousness . . . is only a general term for all our feelings, of whatever species these may be,—sensations, thoughts, desires;—in short, all those states or affections of mind in which the phenomena of mind consist." And Mackintosh in 1830 makes the "distinction between the percipient and what, perhaps, we may venture to call the emotive or pathematic part of human nature."[13]

Of course under these generalizations there was going on a great deal of debate concerning exact relationships, but how little these rise to the surface of current usage is indicated by the New English Dictionary's own generalizations which, though they cover Fechner, James, McDougall, still interweave the familiar words. One of its definitions of feeling is the "condition of being emotionally affected"; one definition of emotion, "a mental 'feeling' or 'affection'"; one of passion, "an affection of the mind"; and always the examples, "ambition, avarice, desire, hope, fear."

The vocabulary as it came to Wordsworth from the eighteenth century had both this general import and some specializations from philosophers like Hartley. Professor Beatty's study of Wordsworth[14] is notable for its analysis of these specific meanings, the

[12] B. N. Defoe, *A Compleat English Dictionary.*
[13] These from NED. See also chapters on emotion and language by Henry Home, Lord Kames, *Elements of Criticism,* chaps. ii, xvii, and App.
[14] Arthur Beatty, *William Wordsworth, His Doctrine and Art in Their Historical Relations,* 2d ed.

Hartleian structure, for example, building from sensations and ideas to feelings, thence into controlling affections, and finally into the moral happiness which crowned the whole. But Wordsworth, as the proportions in the Concordance show (see table 4), dealt only on special occasions with these words in the balances and patterns provided by philosophy; he used *love* far more than any other single word, except *man, life,* and the common verbs, and the other terms of emotion in order, *hope, fear, joy, pleasure* and its variations, *care, happy, pride,* and so forth, in all their abundance, without particular regard for preserving the combinations or the antitheses of the theorists. What is of importance to a study of the word material as a whole, rather than of the orderly ideas it sometimes stood for, is that its most common connections in the poetry are explained by some of the ordinary notions Wordsworth inherited: the location of the passions in body, mind, soul, for example; the working from simple to complex, the basis in pleasure and pain and their contrast, the universality of the passions and their ruling force and their proper connection with moral action. These were simply accepted notions of strong value at that time, seeming precise enough. Even in view of our shifted horizons they seem precise enough; we can still follow Coleridge's instruction to understand passion in Wordsworth in its most general sense—an excited state of the feelings and faculties.[15]

The vocabulary of emotion as a strand of poetic material is therefore not arbitrarily discerned, but historically constituted. The passions were entities for the eighteenth century, and their names and signs represented them; though the systems in which

---

[15] *Biographia Literaria,* XVIII. This warning was necessary because among the common people passion had the specialized meaning of anger; cf. Johnson's Dictionary. That Wordsworth usually employed the general rather than the specialized meaning is an indication of his concept of "real" language as that which was simple and general, not that narrowed by a class.

In connection with Coleridge, I should say that his absence from this study is necessitated by his own importance. His view of Wordsworth is so singular and substantial as to require its own study. It is reflected in many of the opinions stated by later critics in chapter ii. It is not what one could call "typical" of its time.

they function are now considerably more complex and their significances consequently less self-dependent, still in simple use the names and signs still represent the passions. For such study as this there is no advantage in complicating the situation as Richards does by his addition of such terms of reaction as indicate either valuations like *ugly, pretty, horrible,* or states like *calm, vast, intense.*[16] Such classifications are illuminating, but on the one hand they may not be sufficiently subtle for contemporary discriminations, and on the other they carry us beyond the eighteenth and nineteenth centuries, which were just engaged in making up their minds about the underlying assumptions. Concerning the material of emotion which is recognized by the simple, the historical, and the general view there need be no hesitation: it contains the class terms *feeling, passion, affection, mood,* and so forth; the special terms *love, hate, fear,* and so forth; and such signs as *tears* and *laughter.*

Appearing with regularity and abundance in Wordsworth's poetry, these comprise a strand of material which in its own variations, fixity and flexibility, and employment of device contains much of the nature of the poetry as a whole. By their appearances and usual contexts and shapes the terms make plain both their traditional associations and the personal flavor they had for Wordsworth. When they came to his mind they came with certain accepted ties, or with innovations in ties of his own.

The next question is, then, How do the names of emotions appear, in what immediate contexts?[17] What are the proportions of their chief types of appearance? For example, it may be noted that half of Wordsworth's words of emotion are used singly, in phrases where no further modification of them is made by addition or qualification, by analogy or location. Instances of such

---

[16] Richards, *Practical Criticism,* pp. 217–222.

[17] I use the term *context* in its usual sense, not in the sense suggested by Richards in *Interpretation in Teaching,* p. viii. His distinction between *context* and *setting* is a valuable one, but the application of the terms seems to me too contrary to usage.

appearance are lines we have already seen: "That there was pleasure there," "Have I not reason to lament," or still more simply, "he loved," "he danced with glee," "he wept." In a measure, of course, every one of these words modifies every other, but since our interest is in the poetic character of the emotion as Wordsworth saw it, we may call single any word of emotion not directly characterized.

The means of direct characterization seem to be five. One is what may be called "general"—it uses adjective, apposition, repetition, listing, or some form of punctuational stress to set off the named emotion. Examples from the *Lyrical Ballads* are "Vital feelings of delight," "in the milder grief of pity," "Of hardship, skill or courage, joy or fear," "Oh misery! oh misery!" A further stage of complexity and stress is arrived at when the emotions become subject or theme for a few lines and take in a wider area of expressed connections:

> A temper known to those, who, after long
> And weary expectation, have been blest
> With sudden happiness beyond all hope.

Or:

> Never to blend our pleasure or our pride
> With sorrow of the meanest thing that feels.

A second means of building up the emotion is that of locating it in the place it is felt—in the body, in the heart. By this device its physical power rather than its abstract force is stressed:

> In hours of weariness, sensations sweet,
> Felt in the blood, and felt along the heart, ...

The physical signs of feeling—tears, laughter, and the beating of the heart itself—may be included here. In "Michael" are a multitude of hearts, *light heart, recovered heart, proud heart, full heart, rejoicing heart,* all these and more.

To a third device we may give, as Wordsworth by implication gave, the label "bestowal." Here is an alternative kind of location—not in the human body where the feeling seems to belong, but in the outer world, where it is placed by transference, by "bestowal."[18] One will note from such examples as "every flower Enjoys the air it breathes," "the magpie chatters with delight," and

> The stars had feelings which they sent
> Into those favoured bowers . . .

that what was Wordsworth's favorite was later to become part of Ruskin's condemned "pathetic fallacy." The rivulet delighting, the budding groves eager, have a feeling which is a part of Wordsworth, yet expressly exterior; it is a relationship fully described in the first books of the *Prelude*, characteristic of his mind and composition, neither of true fusion on the one hand nor of mechanical binding on the other. It is perhaps a transitional relationship significant in English poetry.

The fourth and fifth contexts of elaboration are devices of analogy. One is personification, as in "time is a true friend to sorrow" (the device is not strongly used in the *Lyrical Ballads*); the other, objectification, as in "the food of pride," "links of love," "the engines of her pain," whereby the emotion by metaphor receives some of the characteristics or relationships of the outer objects.

Wordsworth, then, enlarges, amplifies, specifies his stated emotion in the ways in which he thinks of it: as abstract force, as physically felt force, as shared with nature, as having human forms and objects' qualities. The proportions of these tend to be, in the *Lyrical Ballads*, and also in his work as a whole, the general, one third; the physical, one third; and the other three together, one third, with personification the weakest and be-

---

[18] As in a letter concerning "The White Doe," in *Letters: the Middle Years*, ed. Ernest de Selincourt, II:705: "Throughout, objects . . . derive their influence not from properties inherent in them, . . . but from such as are bestowed upon them by the minds of those who are conversant with or affected by those objects. Thus the Poetry, if there be any in the work, proceeds whence it ought to do, from the soul of Man, communicating its creative energies to the images of the external world.

stowal the strongest of these last. The proportions, the relation of these elaborated statements to the larger unelaborated group, the whole pattern in numerical terms, are set down in table 1 in the Appendix to the present study. What is important to recognize here is, first, that Wordsworth used his words of emotion in large part without amplification, seeming to rely on the plain sense of "the sight made him happy" to convey a poetic weight of meaning; and second, that when he did elaborate upon his terms, about half the time, he did so in certain main ways, having apparently some clear vision of what was fit, poetic, and true to be said about an emotion.

We have some sense of the words and the immediate contexts as recognizable, then. The further questions concern amount and relative consistency of appearance. We have seen in three representative poems of the *Lyrical Ballads* that named, stated, emotion seemed to occur regularly in the course of the larger statement. That is true of the *Lyrical Ballads* as a whole, and it is true also of Wordsworth's *Poetical Works* as a whole. The figures are these (see table 1):

In the 4900 lines of the *Lyrical Ballads* there are 750 names of emotion, that is, 750 single words naming emotion and its signs. This amounts to an occurrence of such statement once in every 7 lines. In the 53,000 lines of the total *Poetical Works* there are about 9000 statements, or one in 6 lines. In no single published group, like the *Lyrical Ballads,* like the *Prelude, Recluse, Excursion, White Doe, River Duddon, Ecclesiastical Sonnets,* the poems of 1801–1807, of 1808–1820, of 1823–1837, of 1838–1847, does the frequency vary far from this, being always once in 5, 6, or 7 lines.

Further, no single one of the fifty-six Lyrical Ballads of 1800 lacks statement. Some have as few as one in 30 lines, but most are near the average. The same is true for the complete poetical works, with the exception of some dozen poems, chiefly in the later *Tours* series, which omit the naming of emotion altogether.

Since these amount to but a fraction of 1 per cent of the total, and since their omissions are only partial, as within a series, they do not indicate the tendency toward creating implied emotional tension that we might wish to see in them. On the whole, then, from the earliest lyrics to the latest occasional verses in the 1840's, from the rambling humor of "The Waggoner" to the firm exercise of the Ecclesiastical Sonnets, from the "Lucy" poems to the reports of "Tours," the names of the emotions provided the solid substance of the poetry at a rate of once every 6 lines, both as total frequency and as frequency in most of the poems long or short. The poetic progress within stanza and poem unit was regularly from object and feeler to stated feeling. Response stated in simple terms of emotion was, whether by quantity, quality, or persistence, evidently some part of "essential" poetry to Wordsworth.

We must see, then, from statistics even so briefly set forth as preliminary, that it should be difficult for the literary critics to define poetry to the exclusion of such insisted-upon poetic substance, unless prescriptively for our immediate good; and difficult for the scholars, on the other hand, to point out the essential Wordsworth, the essential romantic spirit, without regard for this material which Wordsworth appears to have considered essential.[19]

---

[19] An example of such evaluation, illuminating for its emphatic statement of attitude, is J. A. Chapman's essay in *Papers on Shelley, Wordsworth, and Others*, pp. 19–39. His objection is that Wordsworth catalogues, does not present, uses too often a denotative, logical, nonpoetic method. Thus he finds nothing in Wordsworth's poetry equal in power of revelation to

> " 'Wrap thy form in a mantle grey,
> Star-inwrought!
> Blind with thine hair the eyes of day,'

But then such utterances contain for me almost the whole possible range of Nature poetry, just as I cannot conceive of anything more charged with all the poetry of speech than:

> ' the fleecy star that bears
> Andromeda far off Atlantic seas.' "

Others making such comment are Hugh I'A. Fausset, *The Lost Leader*, p. 13; H. W. Garrod, *Wordsworth*, 2d ed., p. 35; H. F. Sampson, *The Language of Poetry*, pp. 34–35. Some disagreeing as to whether "objectivity" or "subjectivity" is characteristic of Wordsworth are: Walter Raleigh, *Wordsworth*, pp. 114–122; Herbert Read, *Wordsworth*, p. 179; Willard Sperry, *Wordsworth's Anti-Climax*, p. 22. And a warning to the biographers, on like grounds of selectivity, is well phrased by Bennett Weaver: "Surely we are on the high street to the misunderstanding of poetry when we first inform it with biographical meaning and then inform ourselves with the poetical meaning derived from the biographical."—"Wordsworth's Prelude," *Studies in Philology*, XXXI:534.

When Rylands opposes "those bright blue eggs together laid" as typical of Wordsworth to "the fancied supplications of humbled enmity" as typical of Dr. Johnson,[20] he is ignoring for purposes of his own the vast store of deft abstract statement by Wordsworth, far more powerful and frequent than the type of the bright blue eggs. Whether the blue eggs are, however, important to poetry as new to it in Wordsworth is another matter and more important. When Arnold stresses the Wordsworthian suggestive qualities of "And never lifted up a single stone," he does not also make clear the fact that the emotional setting of this line was made in statement just a few lines before:

> There is a comfort in the strength of love;
> 'Twill make a thing endurable, which else
> Would overset the brain or break the heart:

Further, we have other selections. "An old shepherd sitting motionless by an unfinished sheepfold, a gray cloak seen in the distance on a lonely moor—these are the Wordsworth whom we first knew and to whom we always return."[21] Sperry widens Michael's emotion to the atmosphere of scene, the gray, the lonely, the distant, which after Wordsworth's time were actually to become major poetic terms. Read calls "The Solitary Reaper" "the quintessence of English poetry";[22] Leavis finds in "A Slumber Did My Spirit Steal" Wordsworth at his supreme height.[23] Raleigh says of the "Yew Tree" lines containing "Fear and trembling Hope, Silence and Foresight; Death the Skeleton" that "had Wordsworth always written thus, he would have escaped all blame,"[24] while Wordsworth, though he liked these lines himself,[25] seldom "escaped blame" by writing in their enthusiastic manner of processional personification.

---

[20] George Rylands, "English Poetry and the Abstract Word," *Essays and Studies*, XVI, ed. Grierson, pp. 53 ff.

[21] Sperry, *op. cit.*, p. 20.   [22] Herbert Read, *Phases of English Poetry*, p. 100.

[23] F. R. Leavis, *Revaluations*, p. 214.

[24] Raleigh, *Wordsworth*, p. 106.

[25] *Correspondence of Henry Crabb Robinson with the Wordsworth Circle*, ed. Edith Morley, II:820.

So Wordsworth shows himself to be an enduring poet by meaning so many essentials to many men and sounding so deeply like
himself in lines of deeply varying style. From time to time the
types of choice change, and the type of our day is characterized,
in spite of variety, by the clear presentation of sensed qualities.
As our critics are wary of expressed emotion, so they are sensitive
to emotion unexpressed, contained in detail of sight and sound,
and such a passage as the skating passage of the *Prelude* comes
to have the proper ring:

> When we had given our bodies to the wind,
> And all the shadowy banks on either side
> Came sweeping through the darkness, spinning still
> The rapid line of motion, then at once
> Have I, reclining back upon my heels,
> Stopped short; yet still the solitary cliffs
> Wheeled by me—even as if the earth had rolled
> With visible motion her diurnal round![20]

Mr. Beach has recently quoted as a peculiarly satisfying description of nature the first lines of Wordsworth's second poem
"To Sleep," and again it is a poem that sounds to us like poetry,
and again it is of a kind relatively rare among Wordsworth's
Works:

> A flock of sheep that leisurely pass by,
> One after one; the sound of rain, and bees
> Murmuring; the fall of rivers, winds and seas,
> Smooth fields, white sheets of water, and pure sky;
> I have thought of all by turns, and yet do lie
> Sleepless! And soon the small birds' melodies
> Must hear, first uttered from my orchard trees;
> And the first cuckoo's melancholy cry.
> Even thus last night, and two nights more, I lay,
> And could not win thee, Sleep! by any stealth:
> So do not let me wear tonight away:
> Without Thee what is all the morning's wealth?
> Come, blessed barrier between day and day,
> Dear mother of fresh thoughts and joyous health![27]

---

[20] I:453–460.
[27] Quoted by Joseph Warren Beach in *The Concept of Nature in Nineteenth Century English Poetry*, p. 33.

But even the sleeplessly remembered sound of rain and the smooth fields, even the blessed barrier between day and day, are rounded out by the phrase *and joyous health*.

It is possible to say that in this insistence Wordsworth erred, that he was the less poet as he was the more ready to generalize, to catalogue, to state explicitly. It is possible to praise as he approximated our ends and blame as he refused even to look toward them; including or excluding from the realm of poetry by definition. Such analysis and evaluation is in fact necessary, if we are to have clearly in mind our own tastes and standards of value. But one has inklings, as when one finds in Wordsworth's prose note rather than his poem the qualities we call poetic, of other and totally different standards of value by which poetry has been written. And if, as one supposes, the standards are exemplified in the products, then the poetry has a meaning other than our meaning.

Virginia Woolf has suggested that "the weather has varied almost as much in the course of generations as has mankind. The snow of those days was more formally shaped and a good deal softer than the snow of ours, just as an 18th century cow was no more like our cows than she was like the florid and fiery cows of Elizabethan pastures."[28] And if the concepts change, the powers and persons of the words do also, the words rise and fall in weight and price, and shift, as their places of general significance shift, in suitability to poetry.

> Ye know eek that in form of speech is chaunge
> Within a thousand year, and wordes tho
> That hadden pris, now wonder nice and straunge
> Us thinketh hem; and yit they spake hem so.[29]

As for the words of emotion, they have had their standards for presence or absence. In the fourteenth-century ballad of "The

[28] *The Common Reader*, p. 259.
[29] Geoffrey Chaucer, "Troilus and Cressida," II, ll. 22–25.

Cruel Brother," a lady was wooed and wed, stabbed by her brother, mounted to go a journey, lighted down to bleed awhile and to make her will with no more statement than " a heigh ho and a lillie gay."[30] In Shakespeare the memorable statements are innumerable. In Pope there is skill and abundance. In the nineteenth century, Empson suggests, there is the implication that one is too exhausted by the wealth of experience to say or feel positively, and

The corresponding thing at present is to express quite strong feelings in a placid way, but feelings such as would only have occurred to a very active and informed sensibility, so that to the auditor they seem impressively inappropriate.[31]

What one turns to, with all the aid of criticism and biography and social history, is the plain substance of the poetry as it is written and the plain intention of the poet—if he has one formed.

Wordsworth seems to me to have made such formulation with vigor and consistency. The *Lyrical Ballads* themselves, even without their explanatory and troubleworthy Prefaces, indicate intention by their material. A single poem, such as "The Thorn" with its two notes of comment, serves as compact example of theory and practice together. In one of these notes Wordsworth defends the repetitiousness of the poem, the words it stresses over and over "in the balance of feeling," by refrain and by exclamation: the thorn itself and the *oh misery!* cry of the heroine.

For the Reader cannot be too often reminded that Poetry is passion: it is the history or science of feelings: now every man must know that an attempt is rarely made to communicate impassioned feelings without something of an accompanying consciousness of the inadequateness of our powers, or the deficiencies of language. During such efforts there will be a craving in the mind, and as long as it is unsatisfied the Speaker will cling to the same words, or words of the same character. There are also various other reasons why repetition and apparent tautology are frequently beauties of the highest kind. Among the chief of these reasons is the interest which the mind attaches to words, not only

---

[30] F. J. Child, *English and Scottish Popular Ballads,* Vol. I.
[31] *Seven Types of Ambiguity,* p. 242.

as symbols of the passion, but as *things,* active and efficient, which are of themselves part of the passion. And further, from a spirit of fondness, exultation, and gratitude the mind luxuriates in the repetition of words which appear successfully to communicate its feelings.[32]

The words the poet uses, then, he uses with "fondness, exultation, and gratitude"; he repeats the words that say what he wants said. And further, he is explicit about what he wants said in this poem: he wants to endow the thorn with some significance, some connection with human feeling. This he states as the basic reason for the plot, the elaborations of story telling, the repetitions (not the omissions) of the ballad form. "The Thorn" was, he says,

> Written at Alfoxden. Arose out of my observing, on the ridge of Quantock Hill, on a stormy day, a thorn which I had often past, in calm and bright weather, without noticing it. I said to myself, "Cannot I by some invention do as much to make this Thorn permanently an impressive object as the storm has made it to my eyes at this moment?" I began the poem accordingly, and composed it with great rapidity.[33]

And what is in the poem to make the Thorn "permanently an impressive object"? For three stanzas, its own qualities and the storm's; for the other nineteen, the story of a grave and

> A Woman in a scarlet cloak,
> And to herself she cries,
> 'Oh misery! oh misery!
> Oh woe is me! oh misery!'

It is a story of *pang, pitiless dismay, doleful cry, sad case,* even in the mouth of the narrator; and the narrator is like his poet in that when he relates,

> "I did not speak—I saw her face;
> Her face!—it was enough for me; . . ."

it was not after all enough, for,

> "I turned about and heard her cry,
> 'Oh misery! oh misery!' "

---

[32] Note to "The Thorn." *The Lyrical Ballads, 1800–1805,* ed. George Sampson (3d ed.; London, 1914), p. 177.

[33] Introductory note, Cambridge ed. For Wordsworth's use of the term *invention* see Preface of 1815 and pages 49–50 of this study.

For the brook that runs down from the Comb, the grieved heart; for the man with the lamb, tears; for Tintern Abbey, memory of passion; for the cold sun, joy; for the thorn, misery. Poetry for this poet links to its objects the names of feelings; and that is the "invention" that makes them for him permanently impressive.

Upon the assumption, then, that for Wordsworth the terms of emotion had an especial poetic weight in practice and in a conscious theory of value, one may proceed to ask in detail three questions concerned with *why, whence,* and *how.* Each of these matters will comprise one of the three remaining sections of this study. First, one will be concerned with the reasons for the poet's liking the names of emotion, the atmosphere of terms in which he lived that gave some significance we do not now feel to the barest words *woe* and *misery* and to certain constant patterns in which these words occur. Second, inquiry will be made into the poetic background of Wordsworth's use of the terms—what craft precedents he had in the era which followed upon the new psychology of the empiricists. What Milton and Shakespeare and Chaucer thought about the poetic force of emotion may, too, have affected Wordsworth's practice, but their conceptions of the term were too deeply embedded in a different metaphysic to receive study here. Pope, on the other hand, though considered the full century apart from Wordsworth in thought as in birth, participated in much the same world structure. Third, by observation of the vocabulary of emotion in all Wordsworth's poetry, we shall attempt to discover some of the relation of individual skill to a body of poetic material, some of the effect of growing familiarity with and fondness of a vocabulary traditionally poetic upon the changing and emphasized nature of that vocabulary.

II. THE NAMING OF EMOTION:
ITS PLACE IN THE CRITICAL THEORY
OF WORDSWORTH AND HIS TIME

LIKE OURSELVES, Wordsworth lived in an atmosphere of terms; in his daily round, whether of walking and talking, of composing or of critical defense, his mind went in certain courses of concept and vocabulary, and he recurrently had certain things to say, and heard others say them. The cross section of the early nineteenth-century world which contained the Poet in the Lake District is open to view in the minutiae of factual, domestic, and descriptive letters, the sister's, wife's, nephew's, son-in-law's, friends' comments and reports, the scenery which by surrounding the household so long grew to represent it, the books read, drafts drawn, indispositions, and what John said to his father, all the repetitions which habit, interest, and the very cut of that life induced. The diversities were bound up for a half century and more in thought and feeling not so diverse as they, in reactions familiar, nameable, and appropriate to life as one could generalize about it. In regard to social problems of agriculture Wordsworth was able to write Henry Crabb Robinson, that friend who was good enough to buy sundries for the family in London, "My own opinions on this matter were given to the world more than thirty years ago, and I have since found no reason for changing them."[1] Except for tendencies toward orthodoxy, he could perhaps have said the same about his opinions in general; they developed, at most, within an emphatic range of facts and terms as natural to him as the air he breathed.

What should be important is the relation of this atmosphere of thought and feeling to the poetry which came out of it, particularly to the specific vocabulary which made it seem for Wordsworth "more like" poetry. (George Moore quotes from Manet an

---

[1] Letter dated May 20, 1846. *Correspondence of Robinson,* ed. Morley, II:624.

effective standard of value [*Anthology of Pure Poetry*]: "Manet once said to me: Vollon's fish are worthless for they are not like fish: mine are. And he would accept no reason for putting his fish above Vollon's, except the reason he gave himself: that they were more like fish.") Questions are, how the poet as theorist writes about the work; what, in contrast to Richards, or Eliot, he thinks poetry contains, intends, essentially is; and what specific comments he makes about poems, so that one can gather his underlying general assumptions; and, further, what is his vocabulary when he writes critical prose. Then one asks how he differs in these items from other critics of his day; on what theoretical terms his work itself was opposed, condemned, defended by his time. And, finally, was there not in less literary communication, in what Miss Wordsworth wrote to Mrs. Clarkson, what De Quincey had to say about Miss Wordsworth, and the *Times'* news of Trafalgar, some of the same atmosphere of terms?

CRITICAL VOCABULARY AND HUMAN FRAME

The Preface to the *Lyrical Ballads* of 1800 is such familiar critical ground that one tends to forget the plain content of its prose. Consider this paragraph—in what terms the author makes his point:

...the Poet is chiefly distinguished from other men by a greater promptness to think and feel without immediate external excitement, and a greater power in expressing such thoughts and feelings as are produced in him in that manner. But these passions and thoughts and feelings are the general passions and thoughts and feelings of men. And with what are they connected? Undoubtedly with our moral sentiments and animal sensations, and with the causes which excite these; with the operations of the elements, and the appearances of the visible universe; with storm and sunshine, with the revolutions of the seasons, with cold and heat, with loss of friends and kindred, with injuries and resentments, gratitude and hope, with fear and sorrow. These, and the like, are the sensations and objects which the Poet describes, as they are the sensations of other men, and the objects which interest them. The Poet thinks and feels in the spirit of human passions.

This is texture typical of the writing in the Preface—assured in its assumptions about the nature of general truth, and expressing with relish the terms of that truth: the operations of the elements associated with moral sentiments, the storm and sunshine with gratitude and hope, an association of object and response one has already seen as characteristic of the poetry.

And the specific aim of the *Lyrical Ballads,* as the Preface states it, is also, and in more technical detail, concerned with the feelings as principles of human nature:

... I have said that each of these poems has a purpose. I have also informed my Reader what this purpose will be found principally to be: namely, to illustrate the manner in which our feelings and ideas are associated in a state of excitement. But, speaking in language somewhat more appropriate, it is to follow the fluxes and refluxes of the mind when agitated by the great and simple affections of our nature. This object I have endeavoured in these short essays to attain by various means; by tracing the maternal passion through many of its more subtle windings, as in the poems of the *Idiot Boy* and the *Mad Mother;* by accompanying the last struggles of a human being, at the approach of death, cleaving in solitude to life and society, as in the Poem of the *Forsaken Indian* ...; or by displaying the strength of fraternal, or, to speak more philosophically, of moral attachment when early associated with the great and beautiful objects of nature, as in *The Brothers;* ...[2] Another circumstance must be mentioned which distinguishes these Poems from the popular Poetry of the day; it is this, that the feeling therein developed gives importance to the action and situation, and not the action and situation to the feeling.

As a consequence of this emphasis, the progress of the argument in the Preface is a progress with constant reference to and basis in what Wordsworth felt to be general truths, and each problem as it arises is solved in these terms. The need to satisfy certain habits of association; the purpose to trace the laws of our nature; the preservation in rustic life of the clear essential passions of the heart; the definitions of good poetry; the discussion of details of style; the character of the Poet; the foundation in pain and pleas-

[2] An insertion in the editions of 1802 and 1805. See *The Lyrical Ballads, 1798–1805,* ed. Sampson, pp. 11–12.

ure; the effect of meter on poetic diction, and the general problems of art in language—all these major topics of the Preface are
discussed in prose rich with substantial reference to *feeling, passion, emotion, sensibility, pleasure, delight.*

Behind the literary prescription and the consistent phrasing is
Wordsworth's controlling perspective of reality. What is fundamental to be said about the universal order and man's place in it
is then "naturally" to be said about the place and purpose of the
poet and the material of art. As the Preface has suggested, Wordsworth's philosophy took some of the outlook and terminology
of his time, with man's response to experience of primary importance, and that response analyzed in terms of emotions. The way
in which man received and interpreted sensation was basic to
general truths about the universe on the one hand and to consequent requirements for poetry on the other.

It will be useful, then, to look more closely at what generalizations Wordsworth tended to make about man's nature to enforce
his points. Here are two statements in the Preface:

What then does the Poet? He considers man and the objects that surround him as acting and re-acting upon each other, so as to produce an
infinite complexity of pain and pleasure; he considers man in his own
nature and in his ordinary life as contemplating this with a certain
quantity of immediate knowledge, with certain convictions, intuitions,
and deductions, which from habit acquire the quality of intuitions;
he considers him as looking upon this complex scene of ideas and sensations, and finding everywhere objects that immediately excite in
him sympathies which, from the necessities of his nature, are accompanied by an overbalance of enjoyment.

... For our continued influxes of feeling are modified and directed
by our thoughts, which are indeed the representatives of all our past
feelings; and as, by contemplating the relation of these general representatives to each other, we discover what is really important to men,
so, by the repetition and continuance of this act, our feelings will be
connected with important subjects, till at length, if we be originally
possessed of much sensibility such habits of mind will be produced
that, by obeying blindly and mechanically the impulses of those habits,

we shall describe objects and utter sentiments, of such a nature, and in such connection with each other, that the understanding of the Reader must necessarily be in some degree enlightened, and his affection strengthened and purified.

These locate the poet's frame of reference and indicate what sort of items it contains: the names and descriptions of the means and principles by which men react to "objects," and the resultant complexities. There is, according to these statements, a complex scene of ideas and sensations, based upon the sensing of objects; contemplated partly by immediate sensation, partly by habit, with the ideas and convictions that rise out of habit; rousing feelings modified by the thoughts which are the representatives of past feelings; leading to consequent associations of painful and pleasurable sympathy and ultimately to subjects most important to men, so that the statement of them in sentiments may strengthen affections and enlighten understanding. The motion is from simple to complex; from sensation of objects to ideas of sensation, and feelings, to the complex in the intellect which by elaborate association includes the principles of pain and pleasure derived from sensation, and the faculties, such as memory, imagination, understanding, affection, or passion, which in their highest development are moral, for the social good, and thus to be expressed by writers for the proper stimulation of their readers. Such a theory, as suggested in these paragraphs of the Preface, puts forward by implication a great deal to be said about the material of poetry. It indicates, for example, regular relations to be noted between object and perceiver and then between perceiver and reader in regard to expression in words; regular progress of relations between object at one end of the scale and soul at the other; regular relation between event and character, between individual and society. The nature of the theory and terms has been discussed in recent scholarship,[3] with most satisfying detail

[3] For example: Joseph Warren Beach, *The Concept of Nature in Nineteenth Century English Poetry;* O. J. Campbell and Paul Mueschke, "Guilt and Sorrow," *Mod. Phil.,* XXIII:293 ff.; "The Borderers," *loc. cit.,* p. 465; N. P. Stallknecht, "Wordsworth and Philosophy," *PMLA,* XLIV:1116.

by Beatty.[4] Names mentioned in connection with influences are Spinoza, Rousseau, Godwin, Kant, Newton, Hartley, Priestley, and the school of taste; and these and others all must indeed have added to the general atmosphere of thought. "When Wordsworth came to artistic maturity, in the last decade of the eighteenth century, literature was controlled by a few well defined aesthetic systems. They formed the only current aesthetic vocabulary. Wordsworth's first attempts at expression inevitably fell into some one of these different forms of literary utterance."[5] "Wordsworth took for granted the purposiveness, harmony, benevolence of nature; and here he was in agreement with nearly all schools of eighteenth century thought, atheist, deist, and Christian."[6] "With this complexity in Wordsworth goes a very large technical vocabulary, involving an exact use of terms which are largely philosophical"—mastered by virtue of knowledge of seventeenth- and eighteenth-century philosophy.[7] The generalization with respect to eighteenth-century systems, then, is agreed upon; the particularities of the associationist system, set forth by Beatty, have especial application to our inquiry at this point, because they concern the very relations between objects, sensations, passions, morals, and literary expression which Wordsworth has been suggesting. Since it was not within the range of poet or layman in the eighteenth century to reproduce the detailed organization of the psychology of Locke, and of Hartley's *Observations on Man, His Frame, His Duty, and His Expectations,* neither would detailed analysis be appropriate here; but the general outlines of experience as it appeared are clear enough, and clearly

---

[4] Arthur Beatty, *William Wordsworth, His Doctrine and Art in Their Historical Relations,* Univ. Wisconsin Stud. Lang. Lit., No. 24, 2d ed. To this closely Hartleian interpretation, Melvin M. Rader, *Presiding Ideas in Wordsworth's Poetry* (Univ. Wash. Publ. Lang. Lit.), opposes the just view of Wordsworth's transcendentalism, stressing emotions and ideas not from experience but from a suprapersonal agency (p. 147). But such influence by God or Nature upon objects and senses did not change the mechanics of feeling; it simply added depth and significance of relation.

[5] Campbell and Mueschke, "Guilt and Sorrow," *Mod. Phil.,* XXIII:295.

[6] Beach, *op. cit.,* p. 13.

[7] Beatty, *op. cit.,* p. 19.

enough like Wordsworth's. Sensations are primary, ideas of sensation generate feelings and passions by association, the faculties are complex powers controlling the simple, the highest powers are the moral, where mind and soul most purely aim for the happiness of mankind. The basis of all knowledge is individual experience, but men are bound together by the primary laws of their nature and the general likeness of their associations.

Look in particular at what Hartley had to say about passions.[8] "Passions or affections can be no more than aggregates of simple ideas united by association." "Passion, or emotion, is secondary to ideas." The affections are a faculty, a power, "have the pleasures and pains for their objects as the understanding has the mere sensations and ideas. By the affections we are excited to pursue happiness and all its means, fly from misery, and all its apparent causes." Pleasure leads to morality, sympathy with God. The mind blends disparate experiences, early transforms "extrinsic" emotion given it by analogies into intrinsic; it has activity, unity, stages of development, and points of high emotional stress which denote its highest activity.

In two earnest paragraphs of the "Essay Supplementary to the Preface," 1815, from "Passion, it must be observed," to "augment and spread its enjoyments," Wordsworth elaborates his creed in these same terms.

> To be moved, then, by a passion, is to be excited, often to external, and always to internal, effort; whether for the continuance and strengthening of the passion, or for its suppression, according as the course which it takes may be painful or pleasurable. If the latter, the soul must contribute to its support, or it never becomes vivid,—and soon languishes, and dies. . . . Of genius, in the fine arts, the only infallible sign is the widening the sphere of human sensibility for the delight, honour, and benefit of human nature. . . .
>
> As the pathetic participates of an *animal* sensation, it might seem that, if the springs of this emotion were genuine, all men, possessed of competent knowledge of the facts and circumstances, would be in-

---

[8] Cf. Beatty, *op. cit.,* pp. 110–127, 153–160.

stantaneously affected. And, doubtless, in the works of every true poet will be found passages of that species of excellence which is proved by effects immediate and universal. But there are emotions of the pathetic that are simple and direct, and others that are complex and revolutionary; some to which the heart yields with gentleness; others against which it struggles with pride; these varieties are infinite as the combinations of circumstance and the constitutions of character. Remember, also, that the medium through which, in poetry, the heart is to be affected is language; a thing subject to endless fluctuations and arbitrary associations. The genius of the poet melts these down for his purpose; but they retain their shape and quality to him who is not capable of exerting, within his own mind, a corresponding energy. There is also a meditative, as well as a human, pathos; an enthusiastic as well as an ordinary sorrow; a sadness that has its seat in the depths of reason, to which the mind cannot sink gently of itself—but to which it must descend, by treading the steps of thought. And for the sublime,—if we consider what are the cares that occupy the passing day, and how remote is the practice and the course of life from the sources of sublimity in the soul of Man, can it be wondered that there is little existing preparation for a poet charged with a new mission to extend its kingdom, and to augment and spread its enjoyments?

This is an interesting passage for many reasons. It describes passion and genius and allies sense and soul with them. It speaks of them as basic to art. It uses associationist terms, yet also combines with them the terms of other schools, "taste" (in a sentence not quoted here), "enthusiastic," "pathetic," "sublime." The parts seemed to unite in a satisfactory whole for Wordsworth. And beyond the subject matter of the passage, the vocabulary of it, as of much of the prose, is interesting, because it is familiar to us from the *Lyrical Ballads,* the names, *passion, feeling, sorrow, heart;* and the mild figures, "yield with gentleness," "seat in the depths of reason," "treading the steps of thought." Language itself, its "endless fluctuations and arbitrary associations," Wordsworth mentions in full consciousness that it is essential to the discussion. One sees more and more that the most habitual and essential of Wordsworth's own associations include the human nature–primary law–passion–poetry–language association, that mention of one of these tends to lead to mention of another, that they form an area of thought which Wordsworth ranged widely and faithfully, in which he was at home.

After the Preface and its Appendix on Poetic Diction, there was written in 1809 an essay "Concerning the Relations of Great Britain, Spain, ... specifically as affected by the Convention of Cintra." That year also a letter to "Mathetes," a moral essay, was published in *The Friend*. The next year the first of the three parts of the "Essay upon Epitaphs" was published in *The Friend*. From 1810 to 1835 the short introduction to the Rev. Mr. Wilkinson's *Views in Cumberland, Westmoreland and Lancashire* grew into the more elaborate *A Guide through the District of the Lakes*. There were two essays for the poems of 1815, sundry literary and political open letters, an address on education, much personal correspondence. No single one of these pieces neglected to speak of the passions of men. In 1809, "The Convention, recently concluded by the Generals at the head of the British army in Portugal, is one of the most important events of our time," is the first sentence; the end of the second is, "what this nation has felt and still feels upon the subject is sufficiently manifest."

Wherever the tidings were communicated, they carried agitation along with them—a conflict of sensations in which, though sorrow was predominant, yet, through force of scorn, impatience, hope, and indignation, and through the universal participation in passions so complex, and the sense of power which this necessarily included—the whole partook of the energy and activity of congratulation and joy.[9]

... We desponded though we did not despair. In fact a deliberate and preparatory fortitude—a sedate and stern melancholy, which had no sunshine and was exhilarated only by the lightnings of indignation—this was the highest and best state of moral feeling to which the most noble-minded among us could attain.[10]

Such passages are simply descriptive of feelings, and there are many more like them in the essay, figures such as the ocean of

[9] A. B. Grosart, ed., *Prose Works*, I:37.   [10] *Ibid.*, p. 41.

eternal love, the porches of the temple, the flower of feeling in
blow; but the basis of these is deeper than mere incidental description: Wordsworth notes toward the close that he has been
chary of practical details:

> ... the whole would have been further illustrated, if I could sooner
> have returned to the subject; but it was first necessary to examine the
> grounds of hope in the grand and disinterested passions, and in the
> laws of universal morality. My attention has therefore been chiefly
> directed to these laws and passions; in order to elevate in some degree,
> the conceptions of my readers; and with a wish to rectify and fix, in
> this fundamental point, their judgements.[11]

Consequently, there have been many phrases such as "fellowship
of sentient nature," "the acknowledged constitution of human
nature," "benign elementary feelings of society," "the instincts
of natural and social man." Paragraphs built upon these phrases
have developed the processes of thought and feeling as they work
universally and throughout a nation, basically alike in every man,
and purest, as the Preface to the *Lyrical Ballads* has already postu-
lated, in the peasant, for "the belt or girdle of his mind has never
been stretched to utter relaxation by false philosophy."[12] Not only
is the problem of international policy literally reduced to terms
of human passion and sympathy: these terms are also elaborated
upon, given metaphor and climax, made the solid material of
many passages. Notice the texture of this prose:

> ... Not by bread alone is the life of Man sustained; not by raiment
> alone is he warmed;—but by the genial and vernal inmate of the breast,
> which at once pushes forth and cherishes; by self-support and self-
> sufficing endeavours; by anticipations, apprehensions, and active re-
> membrances; by elasticity under insult, and firm resistance to injury;
> by joy, and by love; by pride which his imagination gathers in from
> afar; by patience, because life wants not promises; by admiration;
> by gratitude which—debasing him not when his fellow-being is its
> object—habitually expands itself, for his elevation, in complacency
> towards his Creator.[13]

---

[11] *Ibid.*, p. 168.   [12] *Ibid.*, p. 156.   [13] *Ibid.*, p. 154.

And, in summary of the "order of life" which we have been suggesting as the pervading order of his poetry,[11] a metaphor again
using the words of emotion:

> The outermost and all-embracing circle of benevolence has inward
> concentric circles which, like those of the spider's web, are bound to-
> gether by links, and rest upon each other; making one frame, and
> capable of one tremor; circles narrower and narrower, closer and
> closer, as they lie more near to the centre of self from which they pro-
> ceeded, and which sustains the whole. The order of life does not re-
> quire that the sublime and disinterested feelings should have to trust
> long to their own unassisted power.... The higher mode of being does
> not exclude, but necessarily includes, the lower; the intellectual does
> not exclude, but necessarily includes, the sentient; the sentient, the
> animal; and the animal, the vital—to its lowest degrees. Wisdom is the
> hidden root which thrusts forth the stalk of prudence; and these unit-
> ing feed and uphold "the bright consummate flower"—National Hap-
> piness—the end, the conspicuous crown, and ornament of the whole.[15]

I cannot but think that much of *Cintra* was written with relish.
It sounds as if it values what it says, word by word.

The primary sensations of the human heart were not confined
to more formal writing. In "Of Legislation for the Poor, the
Working Classes, and the Clergy" in an appendix to his poems,
1835, Wordsworth writes of "the various tempers and dispositions
of mankind";[16] in the letter to "Mathetes," of "nature teaching
seriously and sweetly through the affections, melting the heart,
and, through that instinct of tenderness, developing the understanding";[17] and just as theoretically and with equally elaborate
phrases, he discusses these topics in letters to friends and admirers.
One of his early letters, to Fox, in 1801, developed some of his
main points, also to be found in the Preface to the *Lyrical Ballads,*
with the greatest clarity. If our interest were only in the points,
we could list them, but since the whole fabric of statement itself
suggests an atmosphere of thought, it is better to quote.

[14] In a letter to Coleridge, 1809, Wordsworth organized his Minor Poems on the basis
of emotions—from youth to age. *Letters: Middle Years,* ed. De Selincourt, p. 307.
[15] Grosart, *op. cit.,* I:171.   [16] *Ibid.,* p. 279.   [17] *Ibid.,* p. 319.

In the two poems "The Brothers" and "Michael," I have attempted to draw a picture of the domestic affections as I know they exist amongst a class of men who are now almost confined to the North of England.... Their little tract of land serves as a kind of permanent rallying point for their domestic feelings, as a tablet upon which they are written which makes them objects of memory in a thousand instances when they would otherwise be forgotten. It is a fountain fitted to the nature of social man, from which supplies of affection, as pure as his heart was intended for, are daily drawn.... The poems are faithful copies from nature; and I hope, whatever effect they may have upon you, you will at least be able to perceive that they may excite profitable sympathies in many kind and good hearts, and may in some small degree enlarge our feelings of reverence for our species, and our knowledge of human nature, by shewing that our best qualities are possessed by men whom we are too apt to consider, not with reference to the points in which they resemble us, but to those in which they manifestly differ from us.[18]

Think what this specifically suggests with regard to the material of poetry. Wordsworth has constantly indicated that the characteristics of human nature form for him a clear pattern with both physical objects and spiritual tendencies; here he states that it is the very generality of this pattern, its main outlines of likeness, which are important for poetry. We are, he says, too apt to notice differences rather than resemblances. It is not only, as he has already made plain, that one can know the basic likenesses of men, and find them clearest in the simplicity of workingmen, but also that these likenesses and their names, that is, the general abstract names of common emotions, sentiments, and concepts, are the materials with which a poet works. This application of his theoretical knowledge, Wordsworth made over and over. For example, in 1835 he wrote to Crabb Robinson, agreeing with his critics that he was distinguished by having, in treatment of "the intellectual instincts, affections and passions of mankind,"

drawn out into notice the points in which they resemble each other, in preference to dwelling, as dramatic Authors must do, upon those in

---

[18] *Early Letters*, ed. De Selincourt, I:261–262.

which they differ. If my writings are to last, it will I myself believe, be mainly owing to this characteristic. They will please for the single cause, "That we have all of us one human heart!"[19]

In 1807 he wrote to Lady Beaumont about

> ...a subject eminently poetical, viz., the interest which objects in nature derive from the predominance of certain affections, more or less permanent, more or less capable of salutary renewal in the mind of the being contemplating these objects? This is poetic, and essentially poetic. And why, because it is creative.... There is scarcely one of my poems which does not aim to direct the attention to some moral sentiment, or to some general principle, or law of thought, or of our intellectual constitution.[20]

Thus such generalities are not only the subject, but the aim; further, they are selected as having value:

> It is not enough for me as a Poet, to delineate merely such feelings as all men *do* sympathize with; but it is also highly desirable to add to these others, such as all men may sympathize with, and such as there is reason to believe they would be better and more moral beings if they did sympathize with.[21]

When a man so stresses the importance of general human emotion, one gathers that in many and very literal senses poetry *was* passion, the history or science of feelings. For Wordsworth, one now understands, the psychology of his time was much more than a matrix of ideas, an array of familiar terms. It was, first of all, a vital part of any subject of importance. It was, therefore, a vital part of poetry, and not only as connected to subjects but as a subject for itself, not only to be described but to be fostered in others, not only to be treated in literature but also to be encouraged in life. It was, in other words, subject, material to be referred to, and determiner of purpose, all three. It was, moreover, and

---

[19] *Correspondence of Robinson,* ed. Morley, I:273. Wordsworth thus agrees with the distinction made by Cleanth Brooks in *Modern Poetry and the Tradition,* and his choice of the nondramatic is thoughtful and intentional.

[20] *Letters: Middle Years,* I:127–128.

[21] *Early Letters,* p. 298. Wordsworth rejoices at his success in this attempt. *Letters: Later Years,* ed. De Selincourt, II:813, 915, 1006.

this is most important, specifically the provider of much of the direct, obvious, literal substance of the writing: the terms of sense, feeling, and thought were in themselves as names the faithful expression of the thought in prose, as in poetry.

NATURAL OBJECTS AND THE IMAGINATION

A second vital aspect of universal structure to Wordsworth's mind was the function of objects as they waked feelings and sentiments. He talked of permanent objects such as lakes and mountains just as he talked of permanent feelings such as love and fear, and both were best found and most firmly associated, naturally, in simple rusticity. The linking of natural objects to sensation and the higher ranges of feeling is an important phase of the world and of art in itself, and about this union of exterior and interior description Wordsworth was no less explicit and no less literal. The poet who is famous for the daisy, the daffodil, and Westminster Bridge cannot be ignored in regard to these, as they involve the emotion of his vocabulary. Wordsworth himself discusses the bond, and so makes clear, even as we ask about it, the movement in his poetry from object to emotion, stated and constant. Let him do the explaining in his own words, he is so precise about it:

You seem to be desirous of my opinion on the influence of natural objects in forming the characters of Nations. This cannot be understood without first considering their influence upon men in general. ... Now it is manifest that no human being can be so besotted and debased by oppression, penury, or any other evil which unhumanizes man, as to be utterly insensible to the colours, forms, or smell of flowers, the [? voices] and motions of birds and beasts, the appearances of the sky and heavenly bodies, the general warmth of a fine day, the terror and uncomfortableness of a storm, etc., etc. How dead soever many full-grown men may outwardly seem to these things, all are more or less affected by them; and in childhood, in the first practice and exercise of their senses, they must have been not the nourishers merely, but often the fathers of their passions. There cannot be a doubt that in tracts of country where images of danger, melancholy, and grandeur, or loveliness, softness, and ease prevail, they will make themselves felt powerfully in forming the character of the people....[22]

This was a letter to Wilson in 1802. Some three years later he wrote again, to Lord Beaumont,

...all just and solid pleasure in natural objects rests upon two pillars, God and Man. Laying out grounds, as it is called, may be considered as a liberal art, in some part like Poetry and Painting; and its object, like that of all the liberal arts, is, or ought to be, to move the affections under the control of good sense; that is, of the best and the wisest, but speaking with more precision, it is to assist Nature in moving the affections; ...In a word, if I were disposed to write a sermon, and this is something like one, upon the subject of taste in natural beauty, I should take for my text the little pathway in Lowther Woods, and all that I had to say would begin and end in the human heart, as under the direction of the divine Nature conferring value on the objects of the senses, and pointing out what is valuable in them.[23]

Is this not as accurate a description of the essentials of Wordsworth's poetry as one could imagine? On the level of philosophy it sets his values; on the level of literal poetic substance it prescribes the very ingredients one finds: as first in "Lines Written in Early Spring" were to be seen, distinct yet interwoven, Divine Nature and the objects of the senses, given value, beginning and ending in the human heart.

The theory of imagination, set forth in the Preface to the Poems of 1815, is based upon this very separation yet connection of object and perceiving power. Wordsworth did not alter his stress or vocabulary on this subject with the years. The Preface of 1815 has so often been surveyed generally as theory to be contrasted with Coleridge's that one forgets to notice how, item by item, it describes the actual practice of Wordsworth's mind and what he of course considered to be the Poet's mind.

The powers requisite for the production of poetry are: first, those of observation and description,—i.e. the ability to observe with accuracy things as they are in themselves, and with fidelity to describe them, unmodified by any passion or feeling existing in the mind of the de-

[22] *Early Letters*, p. 293.   [23] *Ibid.*, pp. 527, 528. See also *Letters: Later Years*, I:65, 184.

scriber: whether the things depicted be actually present to the senses, or have a place only in the memory. This power, though indispensable to a Poet, is one which he employs only in submission to necessity, and never for a continuance of time: as its exercise supposes all the higher qualities of the mind to be passive, and in a state of subjection of external objects, much in the same way as a translator or engraver ought to be to his original. 2dly, Sensibility,—which, the more exquisite it is, the wider will be the range of a poet's perceptions; and the more will he be incited to observe objects, both as they exist in themselves and as reacted upon by his own mind. (The distinction between poetic and human sensibility has been marked in the character of the Poet delineated in the original preface.) 3dly, Reflection,—which makes the Poet acquainted with the value of actions, images, thoughts, and feelings; and assists the sensibility in perceiving their connection with each other. 4thly, Imagination and Fancy,—to modify, to create, and to associate. 5thly, Invention,—by which characters are composed out of materials supplied by observation; whether of the Poet's own heart and mind, or of external life and nature; and such incidents and situations produced as are most impressive to the imagination, and most fitted to do justice to the characters, sentiments, and passions, which the poet undertakes to illustrate. And lastly, Judgment,—to decide how and where, and in what degree, each of these faculties ought to be exerted; . . .

These are simply the processes by which the mind assimilates and orders sensations: the mind observes; reacts in feeling; organizes and evaluates; modifies, creates, and associates; and judges according to principle. This order of poetic exercise is literally meant, with the separate phases to be evident in the poetry. Observation and description, for example, mean literally "eye on the object." Most of Wordsworth's notes to his poems have for their purpose the establishing of the exact occasion, and many speak in such terms as: "on such a morning and precisely with such objects before my eyes as are here described" ("Ode," 1816), and "Not once only, but a hundred times, have the feelings of this sonnet been awakened by the same objects seen from the same place." ("I Watch," 1819).

First of all, then, there must be literal exactitude of observation, a fidelity to common appearance. But there is in this a danger

if continued without exercise of "higher qualities"; description
without generalization would indicate too great passivity. There
is what Wordsworth calls the "tyranny" of the eye,[24] the power
of images to oppress the sensitive mind if not controlled by conscious emotion and thought,

> The tendency, too potent in itself,
> Of use and custom to bow down the soul
> Under a growing weight of vulgar sense, . . .[25]

With the Poet's special sensitivity, which he mentions second to
objectivity, Wordsworth's mind was beset by images, so that the
further organizing power of the mind was a relief to him. He
praised geometry:

> Mighty is the charm
> Of these abstractions to a mind beset
> With images and haunted by herself, . . .[26]

A half hour's roam, Wordsworth said of the poet as child,

> Would leave behind a dance of images,
> That shall break in upon his sleep for weeks; . . .[27]

This was the special sensitivity which in its refinement set the
poet apart from the average man, in Wordsworth's theory, and
which did actually set Wordsworth apart. We have in his prose
descriptive treatment of natural objects which makes plain their
impress in all delicacy of sensation upon him.

. . . or it may happen, that the figure of one of the larger birds, a raven
or a heron, is crossing silently among the reflected clouds, while the
voice of the real bird, from the element aloft, gently awakens in the
spectator the recollection of appetites and instincts, pursuits and occu-
pations, that deform and agitate the world.[28]

. . . We walked up to the fall and what would I not give if I could convey to you the images and feelings which were then communicated to

---

[24] *Prelude*, XII, ll. 127–139.
[25] *Prelude*, XIV, l. 157.
[26] *Prelude*, VI, l. 158.
[27] *Prelude*, VIII, l. 114.
[28] "Guide to the Lakes," in *Prose Works,* ed. Grosart, II:254.

me. . . . I cannot express to you the enchanted effect produced by this Arabian scene of colour as the wind blew aside the great waterfall behind which we stood and hid and revealed each of these faery cataracts in irregular succession or displayed them with various gradations of distinctness, as the intervening spray was thickened or dispersed.—In the luxury of our imaginations we could not help feeding on the pleasure which in the heat of a July noon this cavern would spread through a frame exquisitely sensible.[29]

Further than these we have the report of his own immediate and careful self-consciousness. In De Quincey's story of the wait for the mail coach are both Wordsworth's reaction and his interest in it: the way his mind worked which established his manner of poetic utterance. Waiting for the mail, he had put his ear to the road to listen for the sound of wheels, and, rising, saw a star shining.

I have remarked, from my earliest days, that if, under any circumstances, the attention is energetically braced up to an act of steady observation, or of steady expectation, then, if this intense condition of vigilance should suddenly relax, at that moment any beautiful, any impressive visual object, or collection of objects, falling upon the eye, is carried to the heart with a power not known under other circumstances. Just now, my ear was placed upon the stretch, in order to catch any sound of wheels that might come down upon the lake of Wythburn from the Keswick road; at the very instant when I raised my head from the ground, in final abandonment of hope for this night, at the very instant when the organs of attention were all at once relaxing from their tension, the bright star hanging in the air above those outlines of massy blackness, fell suddenly upon my eye, and penetrated my capacity of apprehension with a pathos and a sense of the Infinite, that would not have arrested me under other circumstances.[30]

Here are the object, the literal location, the poetic sensitivity, and the sense of the Infinite, which together made poetry for Wordsworth. As he generalized sense of star into sense of Infinite, so he generalized his own capacity for apprehension into Poet's characteristic, seeing himself as Man and Poet, and thereby set-

[29] *Early Letters*, pp. 240–241.
[30] Thomas De Quincey, *Literary Reminiscences,* I:308.

ting himself apart from such awaking individualists of his time as Rousseau, who began his *Confessions:*

> I have entered on a performance which is without example, whose accomplishment will have no imitator. I mean to present my fellow mortals with a man in all the integrity of nature; and this man shall be myself: I alone. I know my heart and have studied mankind. . . .

and went on to say, "I am not made like anyone I have been acquainted with; perhaps like no one in existence." Wordsworth, though he too wrote on "the origin and progress of his own powers,"[31] and cried ". . . an alarming length! and a thing unprecedented in literary history that a man should talk so much about himself,"[32] was not one to say "I alone." For him individual singularity was a theme unsuited to literary execution. His work on himself was not a contrast but a Prelude to his work on Man, Nature, and Society, and at its outset he relied upon the certainty of the human traits with which he was to deal—"hoped that to a certain degree I should be sure of succeeding, as I had nothing to do but describe what I had felt and thought; therefore could not easily be bewildered."[33] Being concerned with his own feelings was, Wordsworth felt, being concerned exactly with human feelings; being poet he was Poet too.[34] Looking at other phases of Wordsworth's vocabulary, even looking at some major phases

---

[31] Preface to *The Excursion;* also Preface to *The Prelude.*

[32] *Early Letters,* p. 489.

[33] *Early Letters,* p. 489.

[34] Such quotations as these suggest the combination he found natural:

> 'tis mine
> To speak, what I myself have known and felt;
> my theme   (*Prel.,* XIII, l. 12)
> No other than the very heart of man,
> As found among the best of those who live—
>   (*Prel.,* XIII, l. 240)

> That Poets, even as Prophets, each with each
> Connected in a mighty scheme of truth,
> Have each his own peculiar faculty,
>   (*Prel.,* XIII, ll. 301–303)

That Wordsworth was not alone in such relating of individual to whole is indicated by such earlier titles as Shenstone's *Men and Manners: Egotisms from My Own Sensations.*

of his vocabulary of emotion, one is aware often of intense individuality and singularity, as in the effect of special objects,
scenes, and situations. Men for Wordsworth did "stand single in
their souls," and much of the character of his poetry comes from
this feeling of personal sources of memory and response. But if
we are to understand the flavor of his general statements, an
understanding of the direct universalizing force of his mind is
indispensable.

When in the Preface of 1815, then, Wordsworth listed as poetic
powers, first, objective observation, and second, sensibility, he was
establishing his own literalness and refinement of vision. The further required powers further establish his emphasis on the generalizing activity of the human and poetic mind. Sense of natural
objects is not material for its own sake, it is material for the spirit;
abstraction not only relieves the pressure of images, it also gives
images their significance.

>   my mind had exercised
> Upon the vulgar forms of present things,
> The actual world of our familiar days,
> Yet higher power;

and,

> By sensible impressions not enthralled,
> But by their quickening impulse made more prompt
> To hold fit converse with the spiritual world,—[35]

The higher powers which Wordsworth lists to be exercised
upon the actual world are the associationist powers of connecting,
weighing, ordering, and so forth. They are Wordsworth's versions of the selecting which any art must do. They are distinguished by their interpretation of selecting as ordering toward
generalization in feeling. They require the selection of objects
which arouse certain emotions; the view of these for their underlying significance of basic likenesses, the stripping away of in-
essentials; the view clarified by recollection and tranquillity; the

---

[35] *Prelude*, XIII, ll. 355-358; and XIV, 106-108.

power "to make details in the present subservient to more adequate comprehension of the past."[36] The poetic mind (and for this Wordsworth refers us to the first Preface) has the ability to deal with objects and emotions when they are not present, when they are "recollected"—to reconstruct, that is, to "invent" or create, a pattern from the disparates of memory.

The Imagination, then, as it is further unfolded in the 1815 Preface, is the power which sees likenesses in things and responses, and which associates and abstracts these for their fundamental sake. It is the power to which Wordsworth in all his philosophy and psychology has paid tribute, the power of the general, the principles of Man and Nature. Imagination differs from Fancy in this:

> When the Imagination frames a comparison, if it does not strike on the first presentation, a sense of the truth of the likeness, from the moment that it is perceived, grows—and continues to grow—upon the mind; the resemblance depending less upon outline of form and feature than upon expression and effect; less upon casual and outstanding than upon inherent and internal properties; moreover, the images invariably modify each other.

So lay mind and poetic mind alike, except for that difference in capacity for recollection and in degree of sensitivity, grow to see in every object not just the object itself and what modern aestheticians would stress as its "qualities," but its "inherent and internal properties," those abstractable elements whose presences link it to other objects in a complex of association. As the basic likenesses of men are more important than their accidental differences, and as general language is more useful to poetry than that with idiosyncratic associations, so also the Imagination fits the scheme of Wordsworth's valuation. "She recoils from everything but the plastic, the pliant, and the indefinite."[37] In 1824 this

---

[36] Note to *Memorials of a Tour in Italy*, III.

[37] When one remembers Hulme's prescription, "Always seek the hard, definite, personal word," *Speculations*, p. 231, one realizes part of the way that poetry has come. See also *Letters: Later Years*, I:134–135.

notion of the powers of the Imagination moving toward indefiniteness is elaborated upon:

Even in poetry it is the imaginative only, viz. that which is conversant with or turns upon infinity, that powerfully affects me. Perhaps I ought to explain: I mean to say that, unless in those passages where things are lost in each other, and limits vanish, and aspirations are raised, I read with something too much like indifference.[38]

The imagining mind is the tranquil and recollecting mind, the mind removed from confusions of singularity or evil or contradiction to distance fit, there to be moved by "inherent and internal properties" as they are recalled. The heart's emotions are the more true as they have been ordered by the Imagination.

> Are not, in sooth, their Requiem's sacred ties
> Woven out of passion's sharpest agonies,
> Subdued, composed, and formalized by art,
> To fix a wiser sorrow in the heart?[39]

We are to understand, therefore, that the poet's art must generalize the objects as well as the feelings which it names.[40] The flower is poetic as it calls forth emotion not by its power as a singular set of qualities, but as possessor of universal qualities; not always as a daisy, but as the Daisy. Wordsworth wrote:

"Instances of what I mean," says your Friend, "are to be found in a poem on a Daisy," (by the bye, it is on *the* Daisy, a mighty difference!) ..."[41]

It was Peter Bell's failing that he saw in the primrose by the river's brim a yellow primrose and nothing more; the something more is conferred as it is discerned by the Imagination: the primrose

---

[38] To Landor. *Letters of the Wordsworth Family,* ed. Knight, II:214–215.

[39] *Tour,* 1833, X. See good discussion of the "distance fit" policy in Leavis, *Revaluations,* pp. 71, 159, 171.

[40] As Rader phrases it, *Presiding Ideas in Wordsworth's Poetry,* p. 164: "Wordsworth's characteristic method is to abstract from each object its individuating characteristics, to emphasize its communal properties, and to almost lose it in the reciprocal glow." Stated less sympathetically, as by Ransom in *The World's Body,* pp. 279–281, this method is the characteristically Romantic one of expression of feeling in preference to knowledge of object. Romantic poetry "does not pursue its object with much zeal."

[41] *Letters: Middle Years,* I:170. See E. S. Dallas, *The Gay Science,* p. 292, for early insight into Wordsworth's and Peter Bell's view of flora.

ties. As one is able to speak of "those stronger emotions which a region of mountains is particularly fitted to excite,"[42] so every natural object has its major general qualities and relations and emotional ties. So material objects are important but subordinate, and Wordsworth gives them their due in his specific comments on method. In 1828 he wrote to Barron Field of an objective stanza in "The Beggars," "The style, or rather composition, of this whole stanza is what I call brick laying, formal accumulation of particulars."[43] And to Mrs. Clarkson in 1814,

Do you not perceive that my conversations almost all take place out of Doors And all with grand objects of nature surrounding the speakers, for the express purpose of their being alluded to in illustration of the subjects treated of...."[44]

In the light of his general philosophy, Wordsworth knew easily the relative valuations to put upon experiences, and their proper position in poetry; and by his own conscious sensibility did his arranging and valuing with precision. George Rylands in his essay on abstract words[45] makes a distinction between Dr. Johnson's use of particulars to illustrate universals, and Wordsworth's countermethod of moving into generalities from particulars. The distinction helps make clear the nature of the poetic structure which Wordsworth presents: in theory and practice the observed object, not too passively elaborated with respect to qualities, and never far from type and illustration, given value by the sensitively receiving and controlling heart and imagination in explicit statement.

POWER OF LANGUAGE

The immediate problem of the poet working in such a realm of common familiarity is the problem of expression in language, and the major difficulties for Wordsworth can be indicated by the terms *association* and *art*. We have seen the language of the poetry

---

[42] *Prose Works*, ed. Grosart, II:245.   [43] *Letters*, ed. Knight, III:413.
[44] *Correspondence of Robinson*, ed. Morley, p. 82.
[45] "English Poets and the Abstract Word," *Essays and Studies*, XVI, ed. H. J. C. Grierson.

established by the theory of the poetry, the material substance conditioned by the prescriptions stated and exemplified in the prose. Wordsworth in the Preface to the *Lyrical Ballads* declares,

. . . if the Poet's subject be judiciously chosen, it will naturally, and upon fit occasion, lead him to passions, the language of which, if selected truly and judiciously, must necessarily be dignified and variegated, and alive with metaphors and figures.

The language will speak for the system, and, as the point is made in the Preface to *The Excursion,*

It is not the Author's intention formally to announce a system; it was more animating to him to proceed in a different course; and if he shall succeed in conveying to the mind clear thoughts, lively images, and strong feelings, the Reader will have no difficulty in extracting the system for himself.

"Clear thoughts, lively images, and strong feelings" Wordsworth means to be conveyed in just those terms: the direct images of objects enlivened by illustrative or "collateral" imagery[46] leading to the strong feelings and concepts all stated.[47] It is difficult to understand the doubts of Miss Barstow and Mr. Banerjee and other writers on Wordsworth's poetic diction with respect to what Wordsworth meant by his prescriptions, whether he meant the single words or the word order of the "real" language of men, and so forth. The general conclusions that Wordsworth did not long or at his best follow his own prescriptions seems a conclusion more tolerant of the *Biographia Literaria*'s interpretations than of those directly under consideration. Miss Barstow's limitation of the theory to a theory of poetic imagery destroys its scope and much of its meaning, for imagery was simply part of the problem of the communication of general truth.[48] Wordsworth's pre-

---

[46] *Letters: Middle Years,* II:216.

[47] The order is not fixed. For example, thoughts give rise to feelings, and both to images. There is constant interplay. A philosophical concept is a complex of thought and feeling. See *Poetical Works,* ed. George, p. 798.

[48] "Obviously he is not talking about vocabulary and syntax. Primarily he is talking about figures of speech and rhetorical devices. . . . In other words, his criticism, from first to last, concerns not poetic diction primarily, but poetic imagery." Marjorie Latta Barstow, *Wordsworth's Theory of Poetic Diction* (Yale Series in English), p. 134. On the

scription for "thoughts, feelings, images," means these upon the page, as his references unfailingly indicated and as his literal-mindedness would suggest. Any metaphors and quirks of style which contribute directly to strengthening connections grow naturally from the subject, so that ornament is not exterior. Pure poetic language, then, is that which is most directly clear and universally intelligible, and these are qualifications obtained simply by reference to things and feelings and ideas clear and intelligible, as he sees them.

> It is worthwhile here to observe [said Wordsworth in a footnote to the *Lyrical Ballad* Preface] that the affecting parts of Chaucer are almost always expressed in language pure and universally intelligible even to the present day.

The "affecting parts" are those in accord with Wordsworth's own poetic principles as these are established in his view of the world.

But difficulties arise for the poet, and the first of these is in the associations of words. Some words are not so direct in reference as one might wish, and some connotations are misleading.

> I am sensible that my associations must sometimes have been particular instead of general, and that, consequently, giving to things a false importance, I may have sometimes written upon unworthy subjects; but I am less apprehensive on this account, than that my language may frequently have suffered from those arbitrary connections of feelings and ideas with particular words and phrases from which no man can altogether protect himself.... Such faulty expressions, were I convinced they were faulty at present, and that they must necessarily continue to be so, I would willingly take all reasonable pains to correct. But it is dangerous to make these alterations on the simple authority of a few individuals, or even of certain classes of men; for where the understanding of an author is not convinced, or his feelings altered, this cannot be done without great injury to himself; for his own feelings are his stay and support; and, if he set them aside in one instance, he may be induced to repeat this act till his mind shall lose all confidence in himself, and become utterly debilitated.

---

other hand, "By language he primarily means *vocabulary*, the actual and individual words admitted into verse." Oliver Elton, *Survey of English Literature, 1780–1830*, II:90. An interesting and debatable theory of Wordsworth's meaning for "best" language is provided also by Alexander Brede, "Theories of Poetic Diction" in *Wordsworth and Others"* (Papers Mich. Acad. Arts and Letters).

This is the magnitude of the importance of association, here in its unhappy aspect, elsewhere with positive force, as in the note to "The Thorn" quoted in the first chapter, wherein the repetition of useful words is joyfully defended. Now and again in his letters Wordsworth indicates quite specifically how much words mean to him.

... near it is a valley prettily named the "Vale of Springs"—or "Spring Vale"—what a throng of poetic feelings does such a name prompt!

... three words, in delicacy of feeling worth in my estimation all the rest—"he only listening"!![49]

... What think you of "Columbian" as a substitute for the faulty word—I was well aware of its impropriety—but the sweet (?) sound and the want of a fit term seduced me into the use of it. The word Columbian is undoubtedly at present connected mainly in English ears with the sad sound of Columbian bonds, to which one of Mrs. Wordsworth's sisters five or six years ago entrusted 1500 pounds the better half of her fortune.[50]

There, all clear in the Columbian bonds, is the simple matter of association!—and it was a simple matter. The solution of the problem was to use in poetry those words which meant the same to the greatest number of persons over the greatest length of time. They composed real language of men because they were common in meaning to all common men; they had not the petty versatility of specialized speech. *Tree, mountain, shepherd,* would be such words; and *love, joy, fear, tear, heart;* and *nature, heaven, good, duty;* they are names of familiar phenomena, not deeply analyzed but taken in their general aspects. This is the basic difference between Wordsworth's poetry and much of the rest that has been written. It is necessary to his whole pattern of view, and it is firm and consistent.[51]

[49] From a letter to Robinson, 1835, *Correspondence of Robinson,* ed. Morley, pp. 272–273.

[50] *Correspondence of Robinson,* ed. Morley, p. 237.

[51] An interesting suggestion on Wordsworth's modification of tradition in this respect arises from Empson's discussion of pastoral: "The essential trick of the old pastoral, which was felt to imply a beautiful relation between rich and poor, was to make simple people

The matter was so important that he devoted the first pages of the Preface to it. For example,

Humble and rustic life was generally chosen, because in that condition the essential passions of the heart find a better soil in which they can attain their maturity, are less under restraint, and speak a plainer and more emphatic language.... The language, too, of these men has been adopted (purified indeed from what appear to be its real defects, from all lasting and rational causes of delight or disgust), because such men hourly communicate with the best objects from which the best part of language is originally derived; and because, from their rank in society and the sameness and narrow circle of their intercourse, being less under the influence of social vanity, they convey their feelings and notions in simple and unelaborated expressions. Accordingly, such a language, arising out of repeated experience and regular feelings, is a more permanent, and a far more philosophical language, than that which is frequently substituted for it by Poets, who think that they are conferring honour upon themselves and their art in proportion as they separate themselves from the sympathies of men, and indulge in arbitrary and capricious habits of expression, in order to furnish food for fickle tastes and fickle appetites of their own creation.

Common language, as plainer and more emphatic, as permanent and philosophical, is thus reliable language, least susceptible to the vagaries of association, so that one is able by it to lead the reader from images to thoughts with least confusion. One stays clear of individual foibles and of social limitations of fashion, and ranges in the field of the generally true.

In the final sentence of the paragraph one notes awareness of another danger—the danger of art as opposed to nature. Some poets, by a desire to sound poetic without having an underlying philosophy of poetry according to Wordsworth's standards, think to contrive the sound of art by means of the sound of difference. This is indulging in "capricious habits of expression," and this is separating oneself from the sympathies of men. The fault is the artist's, in his lack of real knowledge, or in his reliance on style,

---

express strong feelings (felt as the most universal subject, something fundamentally true about everybody) in learned and fashionable language (so that you wrote about the best subject in the best way)." Empson, *Some Versions of Pastoral*, p. 11.

but the blame is often laid on the techniques of the art. So Wordsworth finds it necessary to defend meter against implications of artificiality, to show that meter regulates, orders, and upholds uniformity, instead of destroying it by artifice.

> ... the distinction of metre is regular and uniform, and not, like that which is produced by what is usually called *Poetic Diction,* arbitrary, and subject to infinite caprices, upon which no calculation whatsoever can be made. In the one case, the Reader is utterly at the mercy of the Poet, respecting what imagery or diction he may choose to connect with the passion; whereas, in the other, the metre obeys certain laws, to which the Poet and Reader both willingly submit because they are certain, and because no interference is made by them with the passion but such as the concurring testimony of ages has shown to heighten and improve the pleasure which co-exists with it.

"Gaudiness and inane phraseology," one gathers, is that which, instead of growing naturally and traditionally out of the passion it expresses, is connected to it arbitrarily by the personal foible of the poet, so that the reader's reaction to it is one of petty shock rather than of illuminating recognition. Again Wordsworth meant this literally. "No interference with the passion" meant not even such involutions as the metaphysical poets might sometimes put upon it, but rather just "passion" itself named or described in terms of itself, not by indirections. He did indeed like "figures of speech prompted by passion," but these "not as mechanical devices of style."

Wordsworth's standard of the "natural" in language is part of his standard of the real. His most constant criticism of his fellows is criticism of their "gaudiness and inane phraseology," which signifies, more deeply, their artificiality of attitude, the false pressure of art. His specific criticisms make plain the material which disturbed him. For example, his analysis of Gray's sonnet in the Preface is what one now should expect. Every one of the five lines italicized as having value makes a simple statement, mostly of feeling, in general common terms.

> My lonely anguish melts no heart but mine;
> And in my breast the imperfect joys expire;
> ...I fruitless mourn to him that cannot hear,
> And weep the more because I weep in vain.

In contrast, the other lines are made of images created by what Wordsworth thinks foible, that is, not connected with the process of sensation and feeling of objects, but solidified into phrase apart from human response; birds, fields, and morning are seen as if staged:

> The birds in vain their amorous descant join,
> Or cheerful fields resume their green attire.
>
> ...Yet morning smiles the busy race to cheer

From Wordsworth's point of view of process and reaction, it is natural enough that such language be called "vague, glossy, and unfeeling," because it had a different aim, it abstracted a different essential from experience, of outer quality rather than inner process; "thrusting out of sight the plain humanities of nature by a motley masquerade of tricks, quaintnesses, hieroglyphics, and enigmas."[52]

The discussion of Ossian in the Essay Supplementary reveals even more strongly Wordsworth's objection to a lack of the processes of human response. The power of Ossian's language is a power no longer valued by its critic.

"The blue waves of Ullin roll in light. The green hills are covered with day. Trees shake their dusky heads in the breeze. Grey torrents pour their noisy streams. Two green hills with aged oaks surround a narrow plain. The blue course of a stream is there. On its banks stood Cairbar of Atha. His spear supports the king; the red eyes of his fear are sad. Cormac rises on his soul with all his ghastly wounds." Precious memorandums from the pocketbook of the blind Ossian!

---

[52] That figures as such are not unnatural, that it is their detachment from human feeling that is untrue and unpoetic, is clear in Wordsworth's marginal comment on Blair's criticism of a personification of the hand by Pope: "1000 instances might be adduced in which the Hand is apostrophized with dignity and genuine passion. The meanness of the passion lies in this that the several apostrophes arise not from the impulse of passion; they are not abrupt, interrupted, and revolutionary, but formal, and mechanically accumulated." Edna Shearer, "Wordsworth and Coleridge Marginalia in a Copy of Richard Payne Knight's 'Analytical Inquiry into Principles of Tastes,' " *Huntington Library Quarterly,* I:63 ff.

... From what I saw with my own eyes, I knew that the imagery was spurious. In nature everything is distinct, yet nothing defined into absolute independent singleness. In Macpherson's work, it is exactly the reverse; everything (that is not stolen) is in this manner defined, insulated, dislocated, deadened,—yet nothing distinct. It will always be so when words are substituted for things.

For Wordsworth, Ossian's waves, hills, trees were words and not true things because they were not accompanied by human responses to things. Periods stood where feelings should have been, and isolation made for preciosity. Is not the "real language of men" plain, after all? It is only the common words of general experience of objects, feelings, ideas. Regard a tree, and name the tree and the regard, the pleasure, fear, heart leaping at the sight; any order or figure of speech that rises directly from experiences in the acknowledged realm of feeling will be truly poetic, and simplicity suffices. Take note of the Countess of Winchelsea:

... her style in rhyme is often admirable, chaste, tender, and vigorous, and entirely free from the sparkle, antithesis, and that overculture, which reminds one, by its broad glare, its stiffness, and heaviness, of the double daisies of the garden, compared with their modest and sensitive kindred of the fields.[53]

Every grain of these most offhand comments on his predecessors and contemporaries, on Donne, Milton, Thomson, Rogers, Scott, Byron, is compounded of the largest elements of Wordsworth's atmosphere of thought and belief.[54]

As summary of the course of theorizing from universal truth to natural language, no single work is more compact and conven-

[53] Letter to Dyce, 1830, *Wordsworth's Literary Criticism,* ed. Nowell C. Smith, p. 241.

[54] Wordsworth's attitude toward eighteenth-century poets is a typical attitude toward one's immediate predecessors, a mixture of tolerance and intolerance, like and dislike, and a feeling on the whole that he is handling the material better oneself. He by no means objects to what we call typical eighteenth-century writing. For example, he praises Chesterfield (*Prose Works,* ed. Grosart, III:452), Dyer, and Thomson for power of imagination (*ibid.,* p. 465); Cowley for sound sense (*ibid.,* p. 465); Beattie's "classical" style (*Letters: Middle Years,* II:631); and says notably in agreement with John Dennis: "Poetic passion (Dennis has well observed) is of two kinds; imaginative and enthusiastic, and merely human and ordinary. Of the former it is only to be feared that there is too great a proportion" (*ibid.,* II:617). Of greatest importance would seem to be his extracts of eighteenth-century poetry chosen for Lady Mary Lowther, Christmas, 1819, referred to by Richard Rice in *Wordsworth's Mind* (Indiana Univ. Studies).

ient than the essay "Upon Epitaphs," which was for Wordsworth, not surprisingly, a thoroughgoing essay in literary criticism. For him the subject matter of epitaphs, enduring human virtue, was purely significant and therefore poetical.

The essay begins characteristically with a discussion of the basis of the desire for epitaphs: the sense of immortality which is natural to child and man, and the need at once for a tribute, a record, and a solace for the living. Then follows an enjoyment of the beauties of a cemetery, that is, a country cemetery, the benignities of "the surrounding images of nature." Then one becomes immediately concerned with the composition of an epitaph, its turning upon "the most serious and solemn affections of the human mind."

We suffer and we weep with the same heart; we love and are anxious for one another in one spirit; our hopes look to the same quarter; and the virtues by which we are able to be furthered and supported, as patience, meekness, good-will, justice, temperance, and temperate desires, are in an equal degree the concern of us all. Let an Epitaph, then, contain at least these acknowledgements to our common nature; nor let the sense of their importance be sacrificed to a balance of opposite qualities or minute distinctions in individual character; ...

Here Wordsworth sets up at the outset an opposition between the "real" and the artificial which is the opposition implied in all his positive prescriptions and his negative criticisms. He establishes on the side of value the material of general human character, with a consequently expressive language, "the general language of humanity," and he establishes on the side of triviality, or worse, minute distinctions in individuality and balance of qualities, with a consequent language of "tricks of words." The way of thought interested by balances and antitheses was clearly one eighteenth-century fashion, and it is that attitude as well as that style which receives the full blast of Wordsworthian ire.

At the beginning of the second section or "essay," he states formally his theme: "my principal subject which was to suggest reasons for believing that the encomiastic language of rural tomb-stones does not so far exceed reality as might lightly be supposed." Encomiastic language, words naming good qualities of character, lists of virtues, label reality. And, as phases of their activity, Wordsworth defends next monotony and homeliness even to ludicrousness—qualities of his own style which he insists on justi-fying in terms of their essential truth to nature.

In contrast to the "real" language of rural epitaphs is the lan-guage of earlier pieces of mourning from the seventeenth and eighteenth centuries, which Wordsworth quotes. In them he finds two different faults. The seventeenth-century example gilds with "fantastic images," but these do not conceal the honest and feeling attitude underneath. Stripped of its images, the poem tells simply of a husband's tears, and Wordsworth translates it into "natural" style simply by removing some conceits. The poem quoted from Lord Lyttleton has no such basic truth, he finds. It deals in qualities without feelings, in balance and antithesis like "though meek, magnanimous." The structure of a thought which is content to concern itself with the difference between meekness and magnanimity, when for Wordsworth it is the gradation from one to the other that is important, is a structure represented by what he calls tricks of style.

Wordsworth regrets the distortion of true sorrow which both these pieces involve; he is convinced of Lyttleton's actual depth of feeling; but he is intolerant of Lyttleton's expression because its falsity of selection is deeper than the other's mere fantastic images. Both generations, the idea is, were misled by what must prove to be temporary fashions in art; Lyttleton was especially misled, like most men of his time, by Pope the "Posture-master," the man balancing a sword on his finger, Pope, "whose sparkling and tuneful manner had bewitched the men of letters his con-temporaries, and corrupted the judgment of a nation through all ranks of society."

I vindicate the rights and dignity of Nature; and as long as I condemn nothing without assigning reasons not lightly given, I cannot suffer any individual, however highly and deservedly honoured by my countrymen, to stand in my way. If my notions are right, the epitaphs of Pope cannot well be too severely condemned; for not only are they almost wholly destitute of those universal feelings and simple movements of the mind which we have called for as indispensible, but they are little better than a tissue of false thoughts, languid and vague expressions, unmeaning antithesis, and laborious attempts at discrimination. Pope's mind had been employed chiefly in observation upon the vices and follies of men. Now, vice and folly are in contradiction with the moral principle which can never be extinguished in the mind; and therefore, wanting the contrast, are irregular, capricious, and inconsistent with themselves.

Irregular, capricious, inconsistent, these the adjectives of condemnation. The style which they describe is easily recognizable, and its basis in thought equally precise. Its two major traits, antithesis and isolation from stated response, both utterly distort the real as Wordsworth sees it. Antithesis, or the opposing of bad to good or of good to good, or the weighing of characters in balance, confounds the smooth gradation of qualities; and vice as well as foible is individual, not universally enduring, so that it can weigh in no significant balance. As for the isolation of quality from response in feeling, it is the coldest and most artificial of abstractions, since it robs of significance. Wordsworth complains that:

Nothing is represented implicitly, that is, with its accompaniment of circumstances, or conveyed by its effects. The Author forgets that it is a living creature that must interest us and not an intellectual existence, which a mere character is. Insensible to this distinction the brain of the Writer is set at work to report as flatteringly as he may of the mind of his subject; the good qualities are separately abstracted (can it be otherwise than coldly and unfeelingly?) and put together again as coldly and unfeelingly.

Wordsworth's meaning in "implicit" has the deepest importance for criticism. We now tend to call that statement which presents its subject, its accompanying circumstances, its effects, explicit in high degree. We are used to the method, and able to omit one step or another by taking it for granted. Wordsworth was seeing the steps in a freshness of interest which put a value on every one as truth and poetry. *Implicit* and *explicit* are terms which tell more about changing choice and emphasis than they have often been given credit for.

The Epitaph essay has provided object lessons in what it considers bad poetry, so that one need never mistake the brand; and it has suggested as good just what all Wordsworth's prose theory has insisted upon: "smooth gradation," and "universal feelings and simple movements of the mind." Now it also provides an example of the good style, and the style, tolerantly enough, is Gray's, and sounds as we should expect:

> A pang to secret sorrow dear;
> A sigh, an unavailing tear,
> Till time shall every grief remove,
> With life, with meaning, and with love.

The key to such writing, says the Essay finally, is sincerity, which is "inward simplicity," which "sweeps away the superficial differences in things." And the Essay lays final blame for bad writing where Wordsworth had laid and continued to lay it, on either ungenuineness of spirit or "the adversary of Nature (call that adversary Art or what name you will.)" Why, asks the summary early in the third section, does deep feeling not arrive at an inevitably natural expression? "Upon a call so urgent, it might be expected that the affections, the memory, and the imagination would be *constrained* to speak their genuine language." But temporary notions of art have a false mastery.

In a bulky volume of Poetry entitled *Elegant Extracts in Verse,* which must be known to most of my Readers, as it is circulated everywhere and in fact constitutes at this day the poetical library of our Schools, I find a number of epitaphs in verse, of the last century; and there is scarcely one which is not thoroughly tainted by the artifices which have over-run our writings in metre since the days of Dryden and Pope.

Energy, stillness, grandeur, tenderness, those feelings which are the pure emanations of Nature, those thoughts which have the infinitude of truth, and those expressions which are not what the garb is to the body but what the body is to the soul, themselves a constituent part and power or function in the thought—all these are abandoned for their opposites,—as if our countrymen, through successive generations, had lost the sense of solemnity and pensiveness (not to speak of deeper emotions) and resorted to the tombs of their forefathers and contemporaries, only to be tickled and surprised.

So the essay "Upon Epitaphs" follows in concentration the progress of thought which was for Wordsworth natural progress: from Man and Nature to poetry and language, and from the direct representation in words to the ideas represented. In the language is the presence of the meaning.

Language, if it do not uphold, and feed, and leave in quiet, like the power of gravitation or the air we breathe, is a counter-spirit, unremittingly and noiselessly at work, to subvert, to lay waste, to vitiate, and to dissolve.

A theory of language for poetry is of necessity a theory of the wider world, and Wordsworth's mind ranged, however vaguely in the world of knowledge and speculation available to him, with constant attention to the resultant details of the poetry. Accepting the generalizations with the evident meaning they had for Wordsworth, one cannot, I think, be confused about his conclusions for poetry: they are persistently stated and illustrated by examples. And Wordsworth, as one would suppose, did not consider his principles individualistic or uninteresting to the common reader. The structure of the *Lyrical Ballads* Preface as major critical document touched, point by point, upon the appreciative powers of the public. These at the outset Wordsworth described and depreciated, throughout prescribed for, at last made some admonitory concessions to. To the public, near the end of the essay, he named his main points thus:

Having thus explained a few of my reasons for writing in verse, and why I have chosen subjects from common life, and endeavoured to bring my language near to the real language of men, if I have been too minute in pleading my own cause, I have at the same time been treating a subject of general interest.

His topics, advices, defenses he felt to be at home in an atmosphere of terms which amounted to a theory of the world.

CONSENSUS OF OPINION

His contemporaries criticized his practice of this theory in its own terms. For this, I think, they are not given enough credit. Of course, their philosophical atmosphere was close to Wordsworth's and gave rise to the same kind of terms. Some took more stock than others in such theorists as Alison and the school of taste, some were aware of new German currents, some more than others wrote by what they liked rather than by what they thought, some few were more perspicuous than others; but all the variations are visible against a common background of belief, and the topics for discussion were Wordsworth's own. What his friends and his anonymous critics had to say about his poetry falls largely under these main headings: first, his power as a master of passions; second, his treatment of nature; third, his simplicity of style; fourth, his language. They are, as we have seen, Wordsworth's own natural topics. In emphasis, however, they vary with the passing of time as Wordsworth's own did not. I should say that the sign of new appreciation of Wordsworth was a greater emphasis on his treatment of nature, about 1815; and during most of the nineteenth century that continued to be the emphasis.

Now since we are inquiring into an atmosphere of terms, and have in some measure located them in Wordsworth's theories, it may be well to look at them more closely in his critics, to see the quality of their application. To begin, as Wordsworth has suggested, with "the human heart": in 1797 Coleridge wrote to Cottle of "The Borderers," "There are in the piece those profound touches of the human heart which I find three or four times in

The Robbers of Schiller and often in Shakespeare; but inWords-
worth there are no Inequalities."[55] The *Monthly Review* of June,
1799, was one of the first to emphasize the emotion of the *Lyrical
Ballads,* particularly its *gloom.*

> When we confess that our author has had the art of pleasing and
> interesting in no common way by his natural delineations of human
> passions, human characters, and human incidents, we must add that
> these effects were not produced by the *poetry;*—we have been as much
> affected by pictures of misery and unmerited distress, in prose.[56]

Here are two important points: one, that something in Wordsworth's style, as he had predicted in the Preface, seemed unpoetic,
because the basis of critical judgment of the poetic was strongly
in images and devices of language; the other, that "natural de-
lineation of passions" was accepted as right: that was not an issue
to debate. "To you, sir," wrote John Wilson in 1802, "mankind
are indebted for a species of poetry, which will continue to afford
pleasure while respect is paid to virtuous feelings, and while sensibility continues to pour forth tears of rapture."[57] He elaborated
largely upon this.

The reviews of the poems of 1807 again took primary note of
the treatment of passion, but were satirical about Wordsworth's
overfineness. One again gathers that the reviewers were used to
the major terms and objectives, but not to Wordsworth's special
brand. The *Critical Review* of August, 1807, gives violent dis-
praise, on the order of ("if his feelings are not too *fine* to allow
of his holding converse with minds of our gross unsentimental
texture"), and, "He must undergo a certain term of rigid pen-
ance and inward mortification; before he can become what he
once promised to be, the poet of the heart, and not the capricious minion of a debasing affection."[58] And what was keeping
Wordsworth from being what he wanted to be, a poet of the

[55] Elsie Smith, *An Estimate of William Wordsworth by His Contemporaries, 1793–
1822,* p. 2.
[56] *Ibid.,* p. 35.   [57] *Ibid.,* p. 53.   [58] *Ibid.,* pp. 73 and 74.

heart? Why, according to this reviewer, "drivelling to the red-breast" and "nauseating sensibilities to weeds and insects."[59] The basis for disagreement is evidently not the general area of the material, but some of the items to be taken into it. Even Words-worth's choice here is commented upon, from his own analytical point of view, by Southey in 1807:

> It is the vice of Wordsworth's intellect to be always upon the stretch and strain—to look at pile-worts and daffodowndillies through the same telescope which he applies to the moon and stars, and to find subject for philosophizing and fine feeling in every peasant and vaga-bond he meets.[60]

His contemporaries simply were not used to having these par-ticularities draw down value from the general psychology and cosmology upon which they and Wordsworth in the main agreed. They took pains to explain his aberration. The *Annual Review* of 1807 suggested that he starved his mind in solitude and thus attached exquisite emotions to objects which excited none in any other human breast.[61] The *Edinburgh Review* of April, 1808, praised Crabbe for presenting standard and expected feelings in his characters, and of Wordsworth's said,

> Instead of the men and women of ordinary humanity, we have cer-tain moody and capricious personages, made after the poet's own heart and fancy,—acting upon principles, and speaking in a language of their own.[62]

In 1814 the *Quarterly Review* offered a suggestion:

> The man who is for ever examining his feet, as he walks, will prob-ably soon move in a stiff and constrained pace; and if we are constantly on the watch to discover the nature, order, and cause of our slightest emotions, it can scarcely be expected that they will operate in their free course or natural direction.[63]

In spite of this comment on Wordsworthian self-consciousness, the review praises the Lake Poets for exalting "the gentle and

[59] *Ibid.*, p. 74. [61] *Ibid.*, p. 91. [63] *Ibid.*, p. 130.
[60] *Ibid.*, p. 84. [62] *Ibid.*, p. 101.

domestic virtues of an affectionate heart." Leigh Hunt in a note to the "Feast of the Poets," 1814, agrees with the idea that jaded emotions should be turned back to natural emotions, but says that this is not achieved by insane boys and mothers and excesses of all sorts.[64]

In fine, the point at issue was: what is real? The general theory on all sides made the real feelings of men the subject of poetry, but were feelings about a daisy and an idiot in that class or were they not? On all sides "idiosyncratic," "capricious," "arbitrary" were terms of opprobrium, but did Wordsworth's contemporaries deserve them, or did Wordsworth himself? Into the range of an old theory, still alive and meaningful to Wordsworth and his contemporaries alike, were coming new objects of vision, and they were not immediately acceptable. Gradually, however, it was allowed that "primary sensations of the human heart" could be stirred by more natural items than once had met the eye, and by the 'twenties, when Wordsworth's reputation was established, it was established securely once again upon the old familiar grounds: *Blackwood's Edinburgh* in 1818 attributed to him "a thorough knowledge of all the beauties of the human affections, and of their mutual harmonies and dependencies."[65] The *British Critic* of February, 1821, exclaimed, "with how true a hand he can touch the strings of human feeling."[66] In 1822, *Blackwood's Edinburgh* contained a long essay including these remarks:

> Profoundly versed in the knowledge of all sentiments, feelings, and passions, Wordsworth broods over them incessantly, and they are to him his own exceeding great reward. . . . He was the first man who impregnated all his descriptions of external nature with sentiment or passion. He was the first man that vindicated the native dignity of human nature, by shewing that all her elementary feelings were capable of poetry.[67]

[64] Smith, *op. cit.*, pp. 136–137.
[65] *Ibid.*, p. 278. The "Swan of Lichfield's" suspicions of Wordsworth's smaller flowers were finely representative. See Monk's essay on Anna Seward.
[66] Smith, *op. cit.*, p. 335.
[67] *Ibid.*, p. 344.

And the *New Monthly Magazine* series on the Lake School, while chiding it for its idiots, commended it for

... a reflection and abstraction capable of embodying and making mind-created and local existences in the human heart, of those spiritual feelings, excited, from the impulse of natural objects, by the communion of sense and soul. ... He [Wordsworth] does not make us feel the strength of the passions, by their violent contests in a transient storm, but the measureless depth of the affections when they are stillest and most holy.[68]

Throughout Wordsworth's lifetime there were innumerable such comments pro and con, by men of note, Scott, Coleridge, Keats, Landor, not merely the reviewers with their often political biases. Gradually there were fewer complaints and more laurels, but the important point is that from the very beginning the terms and the frame of reference and the bases of judgment were those of general human passion.

At first, discussions of human nature and style eclipsed those on nature, but, about 1815, nature came to be a word more on the tongue, and Wordsworth was credited with it. The *Monthly Review* in November summarized,

... it is scarcely necessary for us now to observe that the sum and substance of his poetical character may be comprehensively described under one quality; viz. a strong admiration of the beauties of external nature.[69]

But in a review of "The Excursion" in the *Examiner*, 1814, Hazlitt had already analyzed this characteristic with greater insight:

It is less a poem on the country, than on the love of the country. It is not so much a description of natural objects as of the feelings associated with them; not an account of the manners of rural life, but the result of the poet's reflections on it. He does not present the reader with a lively succession of images or incidents, but paints the outgoings of his own heart, the shapings of his own fancy. He may be said to create his own materials; his thoughts are his real subjects.[70]

[68] *Ibid.*, pp. 360–362.
[69] *Ibid.*, p. 215.
[70] *Ibid.*, p. 148.

Dorothy Wordsworth wrote on October 9th that she was disappointed in this review,[71] and Wordsworth too may well have been, for this reason: it set forth the very problem of relating objects to mind in which he was interested, yet it found his own method of relation rather too individual. In discussions of nature, simplicity of style, language, this is the point that always recurs in the criticism—that the basis is right, but the poet himself too idiosyncratic. Three aspects of his poetry seemed to irritate, and in a way they were all one. The earliest was his inclusion of minor objects and people in the range of feeling. To that the critics largely became accustomed. The second was the constant shadow of his own kind of feeling; Peacock still in 1820 complained,

> Mr. Wordsworth... cannot describe a scene under his own eyes without putting into it the shadow of a Danish boy or the living ghost of Lucy Gray, or some similar phantastical parturition of the moods of his own mind....[72]

The third was in the realm of language and that kind of literalness which we have already noted, and, because it is the most specific of the three, it may serve as final example of what, rather than his basic theories, worried Wordsworth's critics. Hazlitt in 1814:

> There is, in fact, in Mr. Wordsworth's mind, an evident repugnance to admit anything that tells for itself, without the interpretation of the poet—a fastidious antipathy to immediate effect—a systematic unwillingness to share the palm with his subject.[73]

Lamb pointed out to Wordsworth in 1801 the fault of putting up "a sign-post to show you where you are to feel."[74] Southey asked Coleridge of Wordsworth in 1802 (August 4th), "Does he not associate more feeling with particular phrases, and you also with him, than those phrases can convey to any one else? This, I suspect."[75] Coleridge to Southey, August 14, 1803: "Wordsworth's words always mean the whole of their possible meaning."[76]

---

[71] Smith, *op. cit.*, p. 155.   [74] *Ibid.*, p. 44.
[72] *Ibid.*, p. 282.   [75] *Ibid.*, p. 62.
[73] *Ibid.*, p. 150.   [76] Quoted by Edith C. Batho, *The Later Wordsworth*, p. 117.

The *Monthly Review* in October, 1820, differentiated between the too literal and the too meaningful style of Wordsworth: the former speaks with labored minuteness as if to a child; the latter with the originality of its own thought "addresses the cultivated imagination, and endeavors to awaken appropriate feelings and fancies by figurative words, which really mean much 'more than meets the ear.' "[77]

What I hope has been visible in all this criticism, of which every example given has been typical, not singular, is that Wordsworth and his critics had their universe of terms in common. Miss Smith has demonstrated that Wordsworth did indeed create the taste by which he was later appreciated, by the very tone of the reviews she quotes; but that alteration of taste was within the range familiar to poet and reader alike. From the very first review of the *Lyrical Ballads,* one learns that the whole material of human feeling, of which Wordsworth made use constantly, was as constantly assumed to be proper by the critics. The disagreements were based not on the main substance but on certain innovations within it, innovations concerned with the widening of the range of feeling, the stress on the individual, some of the functions of language. In other words, in Wordsworth's poetry from the beginning there was a fund of generally accepted and valued material, including the description and statement of passion and its whole vocabulary; in it from the beginning also was a body of objects and people hitherto foreign to passion and poetry; and in it finally was a certain amount of vivid individuality and foible in stress of words which, as Wordsworth himself had feared it might, prevented immediate acceptance of the new material.

It is the new material that has received most attention from scholars: the common men, the natural objects. But there remain to be noticed all the essentials of that poetry which were not new to it, which seemed poetic to its critics: the primary principles of

[77] Smith, *op. cit.,* p. 328.

thought and feeling, the constant reference to man's reaction, the general language describing the processes by which everything was known and valued. Every statement that Wordsworth and his contemporaries made was in terms of this material, and it was familiar to poets and critics sometime before their day.

If the basic agreement in the early nineteenth century on the nature of the poetic is at all in doubt, one has only to look again at the twentieth-century critics. They look in poetry for entirely different qualities, purposes, results. They define prose by many of the characteristics the nineteenth desired in poetry. Words-worth, one now knows, was not unaware of what he was doing when he insisted on naming feelings and concepts by the names which now seem flat and general. These were not unhappy accidents in the work of a man moving in the right direction, but essentials of a work which seemed to its author to be moving in a direction of "truth" and moral good which now often may not be called "right." The right today is the immediate, vivid, tangible, or richly associative quality; in 1800 or 1830, most, I think, would have found it in Wordsworth's statement about poetry that "its object is truth, not individual and local, but general and operative; not standing upon external testimony, but carried alive into the heart by passion."

So much for the vocabulary of critical prose and the surrounding territory of thought it represents. One may well be curious, since the poetic terms are to be found in the theoretical, to know if also the theoretical are to be found in the practical goings-on of everyday, the usual words and comments of people communicating and describing in their regular round. Wordsworth definitely believed that the words he used were words spoken by real men: did he himself, did his friends speak them in the conversational letters and the memoirs we have? We may cast tentative lines to see what phrases can be caught, not singularly but in abundance.

CURRENCY

In one of Wordsworth's first letters, written in 1790, the sentences have a familiar ring:

> My spirits have been kept in a perpetual hurry of delight by the almost uninterrupted succession of sublime and beautiful objects which have passed before my eyes during the course of the last month.[78]

And Dorothy's also:

> I have nothing to recommend me to your regard but a warm, honest and affectionate heart, a heart that will be forever united to yours by the tenderest friendship, that will sympathize in all your feelings and palpitate with rapture when [I] once more throw myself into your arms.[79]

And Dorothy's on Wordsworth:

> William has both these Virtues in an eminent degree; and a sort of violence of Affection if I may so term it which demonstrates itself every moment of the Day when the Objects of his affection are present with him, in a thousand almost imperceptible attentions to their wishes, in a sort of restless watchfulness which I know not how to describe, a Tenderness that never sleeps, and at the same time such a delicacy of manners as I have observed in few men.[80]

This is the way the letters sound. One learns from them the health of the writer, his location, his plans, his opinions, or what you will, but almost invariably his emotions. "When I do not read I am absolutely consumed by thinking and feeling and bodily exertions of voice or of limbs, the consequence of those feelings."[81]

As his contemporaries suggested, Wordsworth, the Wordsworth household, was uncommonly sensitive. There are a good many direct descriptions of this characteristic, and in them one sees again the peculiar ardency and facility the time had for discussing natures in terms of feelings. Each is prose interesting in itself for its fine-strung analytical language which yet does not use many particulars.

---

[78] *Early Letters,* I:31.   [79] *Ibid.,* p. 100.   [80] *Ibid.,* p. 83.   [81] *Ibid.,* p. 204.

What strange workings are there in his great mind, and how fearfully strong are all his feelings and affections! If his intellect had been less powerful, they must have destroyed him long ago.[82]

...a man of strong intellect, of strong feelings, of sturdy, massive individuality. If I do not apply to him the epithet "intense," it is because I conceive it to belong more properly to a weaker type of man in a state of strain; but I never met with a mind which to me seemed to work constantly with so much vigour, or with feelings so constantly in a state of fervour: the strong intellect was, to use his own expression, *"steeped in"* the strong feeling, but the man was always master of both: so broad was the basis of his mental constitution, so powerful the original will which guided and controlled his emotions.[83]

Sara Coleridge complained against the Pickersgill portrait that it presented

...a sombre sentimentalism of countenance quite unlike his own look, which was either elevated with high gladness or deep thought, or at times simply and childishly gruff,—but never tender after that fashion, so lackadaisical and mawkishly sentimental.[84]

John James Taylor reported, "...his voice is deep and pathetic, and thrills with feeling."[85] De Quincey explained,

...And that was in fact the basis of Wordsworth's intellectual power: his intellectual passions were fervent and strong; because they rested upon a basis of animal sensibility superior to that of most men, diffused through *all* the animal passions (or appetites);[86]

Dorothy too was described by De Quincey:

Her manner was warm and even ardent; her sensibility seemed constitutionally deep; and some subtle fire of impassioned intellect apparently burned within her.... The pulses of light are not more quick or more inevitable in their flow and undulation, than were the answering and echoing movements of her sympathizing attention.[87]

Such refinement of sensibility and such vocabulary of description were not limited to the great individuals. They were to be

---

[82] Miss Fenwick, quoted by Batho, *op. cit.*, p. 37.
[83] *Ibid.*, p. 37.
[84] *Ibid.*, p. 35.
[85] *Prose Works*, ed. Grosart, III:502
[86] *Literary Reminiscences*, I:281.
[87] *Ibid.*, pp. 270–272.

found likewise in the family's minor kin. Son-in-law Quillinan wrote concerning one,

I know nothing more affecting than this child when he is listening to music that he likes, or to verse of which he *feels* the harmony.—I read to him the other day Shelley's Skylark—His delight was an ecstasy—and though he had been very shy of me at first, he drew nearer and nearer and kist me, again and again.[88]

And Dorothy wrote to her friend of William's little John,

... he is very slow about talking, he has a few words which he sings in our ears repeating them over and over again—"happy" is a dear word of his—he goes about the house "happy, happy!" and it is frequently the first sound he utters when he wakes in the morning, and sometimes in the stillness of the night, he says "happy" and puts his arms around my neck, dropping asleep again in the same instant.[89]

There, in his selection of a term most worth using, of a term of most expressive value, is the true child of his father. In all inno-cence and simplicity of everyday need, that is the word that suf-fices. Likewise in all simplicity his father had written once from Germany to Thomas Poole,

I believe my letter would be more acceptable to you if, instead of speaking on this subject I should tell you what we have seen during our fortnights residence at Hamburg.—It is a *sad* place; in this epithet you have the soul and essence of all the information which I have been able to gather.[90]

This has been a chapter full of epithets containing soul and essence, and they have been of the kind and quality of the word *sad*. They have served for philosophical discussion and psycho-logical system. They have been used to define poetry as a whole, and part by part they have figured in the judgment of it. They have been essential to correspondence, to characterization. They have covered a fortnight's residence at Hamburg.[91] They are the

---

[88] *Correspondence of Robinson*, ed. Morley, p. 495.
[89] *Early Letters*, p. 443.   [90] *Ibid.*, p. 199.
[91] See Tillotson, *On the Poetry of Pope*, pp. 67 ff. on strong eighteenth-century fondness for "sad" as poetic.

beloved epithets of the poet as of his time; friend writing to friend or talking of common event used them because they had significance; though Wordsworth had remarked the fading of the domestic affections in England, still *The Times* used no unusual phraseology when it reported the news of Trafalgar, 1805, in terms of these affections:

No ebullitions of popular transport, no demonstrations of public joy, marked this great and important event. The honest and manly feeling of the people appeared as it should have done: they felt an inward satisfaction at the triumph of their favorite arms; they mourned with all the sincerity and poignancy of domestic grief, their *Hero* slain.[92]

Such phrasing had life from direct reference which gave it power and place. Its associations reached to the depths of thought and the width of common use. It did not yet appear worn or inadequate; it was not yet supplanted by other techniques of phrasing. Life and poetry could be defined as closely in terms of the emotions as Hamburg by that single "sad": "in this epithet you have the soul and essence of all the information which I have been able to gather."

---

[92] *News from the Past,* ed. Yvonne Ffrench, p. 21.

III. THE NAMING OF EMOTION:
ITS PLACE IN THE THEORY AND POETRY
OF THE EIGHTEENTH CENTURY

I s CONSTANT statement of emotion a defining characteristic of
what is called Romanticism? Is the poetry of the period which
Wordsworth began solid distinctively with the vocabulary of
emotion? Is preoccupation with the theory of the passions and
their place in literature the mark of some nineteenth-century
awakening or revolution? This certain strand may well be sign
of a certain temper, and it persisted as we have seen through
Wordsworth's time; did it also gather its main force in his time?
And are we to follow it back, like a stream narrowing and weak-
ening toward its source, into the pre-Romantics of the eighteenth
century? These rhetorical questions, to which the answer is so
obviously to our own generation of criticism "No," rise out of a
long general feeling that intense emotion and the ability to communicate it dawned on the heart, after the dark of the eighteenth
century, with Wordsworth. Many critics have extended that feeling into what amounts to definition. Mr. Phelps, for example, has
said that what the Classicists meant by copying Nature was "to
copy the men and manners of polite society—above all things to
exclude what was excessively emotional."[1] "Queen Anne literature ... was Classical in its repression of emotion, in its limited
imagination."[2] Mr. Doughty has explained that "the worship of
a narrow conception of Reason in the Augustan Age led to a wide-
spread attempt at Stoicism, to the suppression of emotion."[3] For
the Age of Johnson it is further stated that that Age

... reflects the conflict between the two main factors in artistic creation,
unimpassioned reason on the one side, emotion and imagination on
the other. Reason had been the dominating force ever since the middle

[1] William Lyon Phelps, *Beginnings of the English Romantic Movement*, p. 11.
[2] *Ibid.*, p. 12.
[3] Oswald Doughty, *The English Lyric in the Age of Reason*, Pref.

[77]

of the seventeenth century and under its powerful sway emotional and imaginative elements had been repressed.[4]

It has been a common critical assumption that such repression was one of the major causes of the phenomenon which Mr. Read points out: "A distance of less than a hundred years separated [Pope and Wordsworth], yet they seem to belong to different worlds."[5]

These statements and the many like them may be descriptive of the literature of the eighteenth century. They may, on the other hand, be descriptive of the likes and dislikes of the men who made them, using "emotion" as an evaluative term according to their own standards. That the latter may be partly the case is suggested by more recent comments which make an opposite point, comments such as MacLean's

The frequency with which Eighteenth Century writers placed man and his reason at the mercy of his passions, particularly his ruling passion, suggests that the age of reason might with more justice be called the age of passion.[6]

Justice at least requires distinguishing between facts. The eighteenth century's own critical interest in "passion," its own use of it in poetry should provide a little of the material on which generalization may be based. Wordsworth's relation and his period's relation to the preceding century, lately observed by scholars in so many large phases,[7] may be also observed in this small one.

---

[4] Aisso Bosker, *Literary Criticism in the Age of Johnson*, Pref.
[5] Herbert Read, *Phases of English Poetry*, p. 88.
[6] Kenneth MacLean, *John Locke and English Literature of the Eighteenth Century*, p. 48.
[7] Note such comments and such studies as these:
"... [Wordsworth] may have been a 'Romantic,' but it would be misleading to think of him as an individualist. . . . He exhibits also in his poetry as an essential characteristic, an impersonality unknown to Shelley. . . . Wordsworth's roots were deep in the eighteenth century. To say this is to lay the stress again where it ought to rest—on his essential sanity and normality." Leavis, *Revaluations*, pp. 171, 172, 173.
"... Nor was the meaning of 'nature' as typical human experience entirely altered between Pope and Wordsworth, for Wordsworth's peasants were representatives of universal humanity, even if not to advantage dressed." Douglas Bush, *Mythology and the Romantic Tradition in English Poetry*, p. 43.
"... And behind all the romantic poets, it is worth remembering, lies Pope and the

ATMOSPHERE OF TERMS

The scientific studies of the mid-seventeenth century gave the emphasis of empiricism to an interest in the expression of passion, which naturally had been long-standing. The circulation of the blood, newly considered, brought gradually a new consideration of what one should think easily and say poetically about the circulation of love and fear. "That great rhetorical joy in all the passions which we find in the humanists of the Renaissance, and, somewhat chastened, in Shakespeare," mentioned by Santayana,[8] and the philosophy of that rhetoric, analyzed in such studies as Lily Bess Campbell's,[9] extending in the seventeenth century took on a seventeenth-century form. The associations were less of virtues and vices, humours, earth, air, fire, water, mirror, and microcosm, and more of generalized anatomy. The philosophers wrote in terms of psychology; sensation, idea, passion, reason were major terms. Hobbes's first book in the *Leviathan* was entitled "Man," with its subtopics of Sense, Imagination, Speech, Reason and Science, Passions, Resolution of Discourse, Intellectual Virtues, and so forth. Locke, who attacked innate ideas, nevertheless made provision for "ruling passions" through "inclinations." Hume's three main divisions for discussion were Understanding, Passions, and Morals. Hartley involved further the mechanics of the physical and mental structure of man. These and their followers were interested in the exact relation of sensation to emotion and emotion to thought, reason, and ethics; they treated human consciousness as a universal working system.

A further stimulus to that phase of human study which concerned itself with the beautiful, and with art, was the revival of

---

best known philosophical poem in the English language, the *Essay on Man.*" Joseph Warren Beach, *The Concept of Nature in Nineteenth Century English Poetry,* p. 55.

Note also, among others, Margaret Sherwood, *Undercurrents of Influence in English Romantic Poetry;* Eleanor Sickels, *The Gloomy Egoist;* Ernest C. Mossner, *Bishop Butler and the Age of Reason;* Samuel H. Monk, *The Sublime,* see Bibliog., below.

[8] George Santayana, *The Genteel Tradition at Bay,* p. 41.
[9] *Shakespeare's Tragic Heroes.*

discussion of Longinus. How to express and how to create "a rapt and excited state" of feeling was the problem of the artist. Dennis, Addison, Akenside, Baillie, Burke, Alison, and many others in literary criticism dealt in the terms *sublime* and *pathetic* and worked from problems of rhetoric into problems of the soul.

The vocabulary of these theorists was thick, because of the very nature of their subjects, with the naming of passions. Consequently, many statements, many major points, many elements of style in their prose make it recognizably kin to Wordsworth's, and one may well expect some of the same likenesses in the poetry. By 1800, certain fundamental figures in the pattern of thought—the relation of objects to feelings, for example—had received modifications; and throughout the century certain relationships, such as that of human emotions to society, were the subject of constant debate and disagreement; but it is important that they *were* the subject, that interest was centered upon them, that Pope and Wordsworth, for all their differences, had a "climate of opinion"[10] in common.

Wordsworth's objections to eighteenth-century poetry, to Pope particularly, as we have seen, were objections to some ways of thought. The period's very skills for which it has since been famous were for Wordsworth artifices, because they stress the art of the scales, the noting and weighing of good against bad, of ideals against appearances, with the humor of detail as illustration. The humor which comes from perception of a basic contrast or conflict is just that which Wordsworth lacked and disapproved, so that, as he notably condemned the exclusion of new images of nature from eighteenth-century poetry, he also condemned the inclusion of this other whole major material. Both exclusion and inclusion represented a difference in thought about emotions: less interest in the nature of the stimuli and more interest in individual combinations of pleasant and unpleasant emotions. Such

---

[10] Joseph Glanvill, *The Vanity of Dogmatizing* (1661), pp. 226–227.

divergences as these—and all are important to anything that one wishes to say about poetry and its language—are divergences to be seen within the material which was possessed in common. The words of emotion were central to the art of the eighteenth century, as to Wordsworth, because they were central to thought; "... the characters of man's heart, blotted and confounded as they are with dissembling, lying, counterfeiting and erroneous doctrines, are legible only to him who searcheth hearts," said Hobbes in the introduction to *Leviathan;* and Davenant in the preface to *Gondibert:* "... wise poets think it is more worthy to seek out truth in passions, than to record the truth of actions."

Such truth in passions took forms of expression which represented available knowledge—some generalizations about the mind, some major arguments, some lofty suppositions and violent physical images, indicating what was significant to be said. In the prose of the philosopher-psychologists we see explanations in terms which Wordsworth later was to be able to use with an accumulation of meaning.

In their own range, in addition to what they came later to borrow from the psychologists, the aestheticians found it necessary to treat emotion also, because of its relation to the sublime, both in effect of object on artist and of work of art on audience. The treatment of the image was all involved in the heart. When the rhetoric of Longinus is interpreted by Boileau, says Mr. Monk, "The power of the sublime to awaken strong emotions is explicit and implicit in all that Boileau says on the subject."[11] His words are words such as *elevates, ravishes, transports.* Joseph Warton, a century later, was still stressing the imaging power of the imagination, and affirming with equal emphasis, "*Wit* and *Satire* are transitory and perishable, but *Nature* and *Passion* are eternal."[12]

It might be too hastily surmised that the significance of Words-

---

[11] Monk, *The Sublime*, p. 32.
[12] Hoyt Trowbridge, "Joseph Warton on the Imagination," *Mod. Phil.*, Vol. XXXV.

worth's relation to those schools of psychology and aesthetics which in the eighteenth century already used as important the terms he found important, lay in his combination or fusion of the two. Actually this combination began early in the eighteenth century. Mr. Monk's whole study shows the growth of psychology in aesthetic study: that, even as early as Dennis, *sublime, enthusiastic, pathetic* were differentiated in relation to emotion and understanding; that Burke, undertaking his inquiry into the sublime and the beautiful, did so because "no exact theory of our passions" exists—did so by "diligent examination of our passions in our own breasts."[13] And Mr. Doughty, tracing that English malady, the spleen, through the Countess of Winchelsea's ode, Green, "The Rape of the Lock," Collins, Gray, into the nineteenth century, makes clear how all along it was changing from a physical ill to an aesthetic quality.[14] The forces of experiment, of theorizing, of knowledge, or speculation, of taste and criticism, of imaginative writing, worked in a medium which was familiar, and blended where they could; as Burke for example, with his "diligent examination of our passions in our own breasts," sought to solve the problems of religion, of government, and of the good-true-and-beautiful in basic terms of pleasure, pain, love, hope, fear, terror, awe, and their connections with sensation and soul and society.

Narrowing the question to one of criticism regarding poetry, we may see that in detail some of the topics of most concern to Wordsworth were eighteenth-century topics. We have seen that in Wordsworth's scheme he spoke most generally of general human emotions, then more particularly of the poet's special relation to these, still more particularly of the purpose and materials of poetry: thoughts, feelings, images; and finally of the language of poetry: its generality, its relation to common speech and to

---

[13] Monk, *op. cit.,* ch. iii, and ch. v, pp. 86–87.
[14] Oswald Doughty, "The English Malady of the Eighteenth Century," *Rev. Eng. Stud.,* II:257–270.

literature, and the power and association of its words. Eighteenth-century critics touched upon the same points, often with the same kinds of conclusion in view.

Examples of the sort of critical problem that kept arising in regard to the specific subject matter of poetry, what Wordsworth called "thought, feelings, images," and the relation between them, involve such terms as *sublime, pathetic, beautiful, general, universal, abstract,* and *imagination.* For the eighteenth century and for Wordsworth these terms usually were bound up with emotions in theory and in technique. The basic problem was that of the effects of objects, and their images in words, upon the emotions of the reader. The divisions of the problem were somewhat as follows: one, that which opposed the great, wonderful, painful, and fearful to the usual, calm, and social, which latter were founded, as Burke said, upon love.[15] Another, that which opposed the individual and eccentric to the general and universal. A third, that which opposed, in literary technique, the striking visual image to the abstract. A fourth, that which opposed, in language itself, the elaborate to the simple, the uncommon to the familiar. It can readily be seen that these oppositions parallel one another; and the question was, To which side did the poetry belong? Actually, of course, poetry managed to acquire the best phases of both sides, and, actually also, the critics themselves seldom kept the various distinctions clear; nevertheless it is important to note how strongly Wordsworth's case was built up for him by the second of these opposing forces in the eighteenth century; the general, with its range from "social" emotions such as love in the widest circle of humankind, through the general and abstract treatment of men's basic uniformity, to the common simplicity and generality of language in its special center of poetry.

This kind of thought is exemplified by Davenant's statement in the preface to *Gondibert* that the poet should seek out truth in

---

[15] *Inquiry into the Origin of Our Ideas of the Sublime and the Beautiful* (1757), I:xviii.

passions of mankind, not of particular persons as lifted or leveled
by fate—an important shift in opinion from the Elizabethan period. This kind of thought is exemplified by Hurd's differentia-
tion in his tenth letter on chivalry between poetry that seeks to
move passion, which must follow nature, and poetry which is
more sublime and has not the need to observe the rules of credi-
bility of "him who would touch the affections and animate the
heart." It is exemplified again by Hume's assurance that customs
change but basic passions remain the same,[16] that "it is a certain
rule that wit and passion are entirely incompatible. . . . For this
reason, a greater degree of simplicity is required in all composi-
tions, where men, and actions, and passions are painted, than in
such as consist of reflections and observations."[17]

Those champions'of the passions, Pope, Priestley, Stockdale,
Percy, Goldsmith, equally held for simplicity,[18] and in his *Citizen
of the World,* Letter XCVI, Goldsmith happily summarized the
points against the opposition, in his picture of the reader looking
for more than pictures:

> He opens the book and finds very good words truly, much exactness
> of rhyme, but no information. A parcel of gaudy images pass on before
> his imagination like the figures in a dream; but curiosity, induction,
> reason, and the whole train of affections are fast asleep. The *jocunda
> et idonea vitae*—those sallies which mend the heart while they amuse
> the fancy—are quite forgotten; so that the reader who would take up
> some modern applauded performances of this kind must, in order to
> be pleased, first leave his good sense behind him, take for his recom-
> pense and guide bloated and compound epithet, and dwell on paint-
> ings, just indeed because labored with minute exactness.

The conflict was plainly between poet as decorator and poet as
philosopher, with Wordsworth firmly enlisted as philosopher;[19]

---

[16] "Of Eloquence," *Philosophical Essays.*
[17] "Of Simplicity and Refinement in Writing," *Philosophical Essays.*
[18] Preface to *Iliad,* 1715, and Monk, *op. cit.,* p. 135, and Preface to *Reliques,* 1765.
[19] He quoted Aristotle: "Aristotle, I have been told, has said, that Poetry is the most
philosophic of all writing; it is so: its object is truth, not individual and local, but general,
and operative, not standing upon external testimony but carried alive into the heart by
passion. . . ." cf. Preface, 1800.

between the Renaissance idea of instruction now grown into the philosophy and psychology of the eighteenth century, and the equally well established ideal of vivid descriptive presentation supported by that sensationalist eighteenth-century aesthetic which stressed the power of the object on the eye and the power of the eye to move the heart. To confine emotion to one side or the other is the mistake that must not be made. Both schools, all the critics, based every argument upon emotion, its workings, its powers, its connection with objects. But some, like Goldsmith here, did not find it in the poetry of painting of Gray and his school; and some, on the other hand, did not find it in generalization. In the camp of the pictorialists, Joseph Warton can be found exclaiming with fervor, "Among the other fortunate circumstances that attended Homer, it was not one of the least, that he wrote before *general* and *abstract* terms were invented."[20] And Hume assures that " 'tis certain, that the imagination is more affected by what is particular, than by what is general," and that "nothing contributes more to [the poet's] full conviction than a blaze of poetical figures and images, which have their effect upon the poet himself, as well as upon his readers."[21] Erasmus Darwin, whose contribution to the poetry of vision is so intense as to be confusing, has his poet say:

> Poetry admits of but few words expressive of very abstracted ideas, whereas Prose abounds with them.... the words expressive of these ideas belonging to vision make up the principal part of poetic language.[22]

"Gain the heart, or you gain nothing; the eyes and ears are the only roads to the heart,"[23] said Chesterfield; and Lord Kames: "the eye is the best avenue to the heart."[24]

---

[20] *Essay on Pope,* 1806 ed., II:160–161.
[21] *Treatise of Human Nature,* ed. Selby-Bigge, pp. 123, 580.
[22] Interlude in *Botanic Garden,* 2d ed., 1791, and quoted by Beatty, *Wordsworth,* p. 60. Darwin and the image are still waiting for a good study.
[23] *Letters to His Son,* Nov. 24 (O.S.), 1749.
[24] Quoted by Trowbridge, *loc. cit.*

Any prescription that so emphasized the feelings which Wordsworth considered essential, he would hold in favor, and so in his own criticism we find prescriptions from both camps, recommendations for the simple, the pictorial, the abstract, and the imaged all at once. When Mr. Monk says that Wordsworth was the apotheosis of the eighteenth-century sublime,[25] when Mr. Bush associates him with the Augustan Deists,[26] they are not being contradictory, they are simply making clear his way of assimilation aided by a general agreement upon the primacy of consideration of the passions. His treatment of the word *imagination* seems to me a very good example of his method. Out of his double conviction, first, that images were important and the eye was an avenue to the heart, and second, that images were important in the degree that the heart, the universal human heart, gave them importance, Wordsworth gave to Imagination the wider meaning these combined convictions necessitated, namely, the power of human feeling and thought to abstract the significant from objects and images of objects.[27] The Pre-Romantic and Darwinian pictorial imagination was given place as means to the fuller ends of the selecting imagination.

Consider as a whole, then, the eighteenth-century climate of opinion in relation to Wordsworth's opinion and Wordsworth's poetical practice as these pertain to what we have chosen to observe: the use of statement of emotion. This use was fostered by a complex of beliefs and interests the widest spread of which was in the general empirical philosophy that concerned itself with Man through Man's physical functioning, not as mirror of virtues and vices, not as microcosm of elements and spirits, but as representative dynamically of a certain level of universal processes. Whatever these processes were named (such as Will, Reason, and

[25] *Op. cit.*, p. 231.
[26] Bush, *op. cit.*, p. 43.
[27] Preface of 1814. Also see discussion in C. V. Deane's *Aspects of Eighteenth Century Nature Poetry*, pp. 58, 66, of the agreement in attitude of Sir Joshua Reynolds and Wordsworth on the generalized style; also Wordsworth, *Letters: Later Years*, I:185, II:580.

so forth), the Passions were invariably in the basic list. It was natural, therefore, especially because of their vividness in both inward effect and outward show, that the Passions should appear with equal regularity in narrower fields of discussion: in general aesthetic, in painting, landscape, poetry, in religious discussion, in everyday conversation. Simply, the eighteenth century's use of the term *emotion* (with its alternative terms) differed from ours and others' in some major characteristics: one being that it was a very definite term with definite boundaries in the scale of human functions; another, that with all its main phases it was held to be the same in all men, consequently the more definite; and a third that, since it was so plain, both statement of it and exterior manifestation of it could have an accepted meaning and value, so that it was heartily given place in all the surfaces of expression and action.

Calling to mind, for example, the novels and the plays of the eighteenth century, the letters and diaries, one remembers what excess of emotionalism seemed current, to the point of extreme artificiality. It is possible that our judgment of artificiality is itself a little in excess. We now tend to measure emotion more by tension than by spread, and it is for us a more complex set of factors, so that its weight is not now, as it was then, present in its very name. The oceans of tears, the gusts of sighs, the heaving of bosoms, the fits and faints represented moods and reactions with a clear meaning and value to their owners, and if they were obvious, so are most fashionable habits of mind as well as of manner. The large and constant setting forth of passion had a sound philosophical base. There was some variation of emphasis between the lovers of the sublime and the lovers of the pathetic or the natural,[28] but most men contrived to be both. The academic

[28] When Boswell discussing Whitehead suggested, "He had a great effect on the passions," Dr. Johnson replied, "Why sir, I don't think so. He could not represent a succession of pathetic images. He vociferated and made an impression." *Journal of a Tour to the Hebrides* (New York, 1935), p. 20.

88   University of California Publications in English

painters of the period were students of the typical attitudes, gestures, and expressions of emotion, and at the same time the ladies practiced the expressions. Le Brun was an authority on the gamut of the emotions, and Garrick, sticking his head out between the curtains, enraptured the audience by running, with his face alone, the gamut of emotions according to Le Brun's prescription. Norris in 1710 gave the first definition of passion as quoted by the Oxford Dictionary: "By the Passions I think we are to understand certain motions of the Mind depending upon and accompanied with an Agitation of the Spirits"; and before the century was out the novelists were writing, "I tremble while relating it, and have not a nerve in my frame but vibrates like an aspen,"[29] "I could not conceal my feelings, but expressed them in liquid torrents,"[30] "the trembling tear of tenderness,—which in its usual form tottered down her cheek, evinced the soft emotion of her spotless mind."[31] Even Fielding was an ardent "physiognomist," reading the passions on his characters' faces, employing with nice ironic self-consciousness "a tempest of gratitude (if I may be allowed the expression)."[32]

So the practice used the terms of the theory, and ordinary life found notable what philosophy prescribed.

THE TERMS AS POETIC MATERIAL

As for poetry, it participated in the atmosphere with the rest. Its types have already been related in various studies to one emotional trend or another: the funeral elegy growing out of the seventeenth century, the "happy man" tradition of Horace and "L'Allegro," the melancholy tradition of the graveyard school and the wandering solitary, the sentimental narratives like the novels, the musings of moral essays, all reflecting some typical emotional attitude. It seems to me necessary to know the poetry more closely

---

[29] Beckford quoted on *Vathek*, edition of Chapman and Dodd (London, 1922), p. vii.
[30] Quoted by R. P. Utter and G. R. Needham, *Pamela's Daughters*, p. 101.
[31] *Ibid.*, p. 132.   [32] *Amelia*, 10, vii.

than this, in its substance as well as its attitudes. In Wordsworth's poetry the strand of vocabulary made up of named emotion, which was large and continuous, was a strand coming directly and literally out of literary theory, which in turn came from general philosophical theory and a common set of terms. As we have just seen, those terms are particularly characteristic, not of Wordsworth's period alone, but of the years from the later seventeenth century at least to Wordsworth; in that span of time they may have nourished poetry in at least the one phase of vocabulary of feeling to a substance like Wordsworth's own. If so, there should be visible a characteristic tradition of phraseology as well as of interest. Hume himself points in the direction of greater detail, out of the critical atmosphere in which we have been absorbed:

> Every voice is united in applauding elegance, propriety, simplicity, spirit in writing; and in blaming fustian, affectation, coldness, and a false brilliancy: but when critics come to particulars, this seeming unanimity vanishes: and it is found, that they had affixed a very different meaning to their expressions.[33]

But there *can* be standards, says Hume, and the passions are one, for they are lasting.

Specifically of expressing passion in poetry, Lady Mary Wortley Montagu wrote to Pope in 1720, sending him a specimen of the sublime style of Turkish poetry, in a literal transcription and also as she would render it into English. The phrases of the literal translation seemed to her extreme, and she doubted her success in putting them "into the style of English poetry," saying, "neither do I think our English proper to express such violence of passion, which is very seldom felt amongst us."[34] This is a part of the transcription:

> My cries pierce the heavens!
> My eyes are without sleep!
> Turn to me, Sultana, let me gaze on thy beauty.

[33] "Of the Standard of Taste," *Philosophical Essays.*
[34] Pope's *Works* (London, 1886), IX:376.

> Crown of my life! fair light of my eyes!
>   Sultana! my princess!
> I rub my face against the earth;—
>   I am drown'd in scalding tears—I rave!
> Have you no compassion? Will you not turn to look upon me?

Which becomes,

> The heavens relenting hear my piercing cries,
> I loath the light, and sleep forsakes my eyes;
> Turn thee, Sultana, ere thy lover dies.

> My queen! my angel! my fond heart's desire!
> I rave—my bosom burns with heavenly fire!
> Pity that passion which thy charms inspire.

One sees that what for Lady Mary made the poetry English was on the one hand a regular balanced structure and on the other a set of "poetic" phrases, and those phrases, already established as suitable, were elaborate phrases of *feeling*. Excessive as they are to us, to her, as she said, they were insufficient. Keeping in mind that both versions are in her vocabulary, one notes that what the second omits is not any of the words of emotion, except tears, but rather the lines lacking them, as "My eyes are without sleep," "Crown of my life!" "I rub my face against the earth," "Will you not turn to look upon me?" No limitations of English prevented the use of such language. It was rather Lady Mary's own standard of the poetic that made her load the lines instead with the loathed light and the burning bosom. It is important to consider, first, that she deeply admired the Turkish sublime; second, that she mistrusted English; and third, that she felt such violence of emotion to be unfamiliar. The sublime, that side of the eighteenth century which represented the extreme, was still something of a novelty, a little foreign, hence the wonder; English poetry was working more and more toward living up to it, hence still some doubt. But Lady Mary's pieces reveal how far the poetic capacity for heavy statement of feeling had already developed by 1720, so that the piercing cries, the raving, the heavenly fire seemed more moderate than sublime.

It did not take sublimity to raise the passions; that lofty quality was usually distinguished from them. As a matter of fact it was the classical sponsor of the *via media* who supplied Sir William Temple in 1690 with a definition of good poetry that supported him in his neoclassical desire to "raise love and fear." To judge a good poem, said Sir William, use the lines of Horace; he translates:

> (He is a poet) who vainly anguishes my breast,
> Provokes, allays, and with false terror fills,
> Like a magician, and now sets me down
> In Thebes, and now in Athens.[35]

His contemporary neoclassicists, whether in light vein or serious, support his opinion, so that typical lines of their verse may run something like this:

> Still complaining, and defending,
> Both to love, yet not agree;
> Fears tormenting, passion rending,
> Oh! the pangs of jealousy!
>
> From such painful ways of living,
> Ah! how sweet, could Love be free!
> Still presenting, still receiving,
> Fierce, immortal ecstacy.[36]

Or like these of Thomas Tickell, given "a high place among the minor poets" by Dr. Johnson,[37] to Mr. Addison on his tragedy of Cato:

> How do our souls with generous pleasure glow!
> Our hearts exulting, while our eyes o'erflow,
> When thy firm hero stands beneath the weight
> Of all his sufferings venerably great;
> Rome's poor remains still sheltering by his side,
> With conscious virtue, and becoming pride!

---

[35] *Works* (London, 1814), III:418.

[36] By George Granville, Lord Lansdowne, "To Myra"; cf. Chalmers, *The Works of the English Poets*, XI:23.

[37] Chalmers, *op. cit.*, XI:99, 106.

Parnell and Pomfret are classed by Courthope in the school of Pope; they were translators of the classics and men of moderation; some of their works are these: by Parnell, along with "The Flies: An Eclogue," and "On Mrs. Arabella Fermor Leaving London," also "Hymn to Contentment," "The Soul in Sorrow," "The Happy Man," "The Way to Happiness," "Ecstasy,"

> Oh, strange enjoyment of a bliss unseen!
> Oh, ravishment! Oh, sacred rage within!
> Tumultuous pleasure, rais'd on peace of mind,
> Sincere, excessive, from the world refin'd![38]

and by Pomfret: "Love Triumphant over Reason," and "Reason, A Poem," 1700, in which latter, after the figure of reason as a flickering candle and passions as raging billows, he asked how could be withstood "Th' impetuous torrent of the boiling blood."[39]

This question may arise: If these poets are called neoclassicists, if they are practiced in Latin and Greek translation, may not their statement of emotion be characteristic, not of eighteenth-century poetics, but of classical? The problem of the relation of eighteenth-century to classical vocabulary is a complicated and interesting one, but for our immediate purposes an answer is to be found in such a poetic translation as Richard Savage's "E Graeco Ruf"; like Lady Mary Wortley Montagu's, the English rendition provides a good many of its own requirements:

> Qui te videt beatus est,
> Beatior qui audiet,
> Qui basiat semi-deus est.
> Qui te potitur est deus.

The foregoing lines paraphrased:

> Happy the man, who, in thy sparkling eyes,
>   His amorous wishes sees, reflecting, play;
> Sees little laughing cupids, glancing, rise,
>   And, in soft-swimming languor, die away.

---

[38] Chalmers, *op. cit.*, IX:404.
[39] *Ibid.*, VIII:334.

Still happier he! to whom thy meanings roll
   In sounds which love, harmonious love, inspire;
On his charm'd ear sits, rapt, his listening soul,
   Till admiration form intense desire.

Half-deity is he who warm may press
   Thy lip, soft swelling to the kindling kiss;
And may that lip assentive warmth express,
   Till love draw willing love to ardent bliss.

Circling thy waist, and circled in thy arms,
   Who, melting on thy mutual-melting breast,
Entranc'd enjoys love's whole luxurious charms,
   Is all a god!—is of all Heaven possest.[40]

It pleased the eighteenth-century poet to write like this; at least
he wrote like this often, from which I draw the conclusion that
it pleased him. Feelings were for him a field open to strong elaboration in its own right; feelings were a subject of scope and significance, which provided its own vocabulary in amplitude and
enthusiasm. Notice the nature of the language: first of all, the
emotion has physical metaphor in certain regular forms such as
kindling and *melting,* as if the physical reaction had certain limited and prescribable phases, universal in application. Second, the
emotion is given an effect of external power by the *wishes,* the
cupids, the *soul,* and all the feelings which are the active subjects
of verbs. The frame of man has a tendency to be the ground
where such forces play decoratively, langorously, or ferociously,
but always under their own power. Third, the statements seem
to us overstatements, the very combination of two or three of the
words of ardor seems excessive; but I think this was the excess
of interest and enjoyment. The active description of the passions
was new and challenging and absorbing to a poet who desired
to contribute delight and moral advantage and contemporary
emphasis to literature. Or, if you would say that the ardent bosom
and its associates were mere cliché, still why? They were not very

---

[40] *Ibid.,* XI:337.

old; they were not in the love poetry of Shakespeare's sonnets, or of Donne; that they achieved poetic place so quickly may be a tribute to their own vitality as well as to the conventionality of their poets. If one gives the Augustans credit for reason, one cannot very well attribute their enthusiasm for the passions in poetry to mere blind acceptance.

It is true that to quote Savage is to get on in the century to the point where the sublime was outdoing its Augustan efforts. His "The Wanderer" contains so many ice-bound bosoms, decaying spirits, and frenzies of anguish that one would expect Dr. Johnson to balk; but rather Dr. Johnson quotes those very passages, and commends Savage because he "had treasured in his mind all the different combinations of passions, and the innumerable mixtures of vice and virtue, which distinguish one character from another."[11] And indeed Savage did write poems which, more than "The Wanderer," we think of in the school of Pope, such as "Of Public Spirit in Regard to Public Words, An Epistle to His Royal Highness Frederic Prince of Wales," dealing, as he stated in the Contents, with practical subjects: "Of reservoirs and their use; of drawing fens, and building bridges, cutting canals, repairing harbors . . . ; of commerce; of public roads; of public buildings"; and so forth. Yet much of it sounds like this,

> Quick passions change alternate on her face;
> Her diction music, as her action grace.
> Instant we catch her terrour-giving cares,
> Pathetic sighs and pity moving teares;
> Instant we catch her generous glow of soul,
> Till one great striking moral crowns the whole.[12]

In 1753, Wilkie's classical epic in heroic couplets, *The Epigoniad,* contained a good supply of lines like: "rage and jealousy divide the breast," "Compassion's keenest touch my bosom thrill'd; My eyes a flood of melting sorrow fill'd," and

---

[11] Chalmers, *op. cit.,* XI:259.
[12] *Ibid.,* XI:326.

> My veins yet freeze with horror and affright!
> I thought that, all forsaken and alone,
> Pensive I wander'd far through ways unknown;
> A gloomy twilight, neither night nor day,
> Frown'd on my steps, and sadden'd all the way:[43]

And on the other hand, Christopher Smart, who is classed among the rebels, the poets of newer vision, was writing in very much the same vocabulary:

> Say, must these tears forever flow,
>   Can I from patience learn content,
> While solitude still nurses woe,
>   And leaves me leisure to lament.
>
> My guardian see!—who wards off peace,
>   Whose cruelty is his employ,
> Who bids the tongue of transport cease
>   And stops each avenue to joy.[44]

The parallel modes of sublime and normal thus extended into the second half of the century as complements to each other, as they had been in the Augustan period; the golden mean of the classical was enlivened by the vast, the vast was seen through the general eyes of general humanity and thereby kept out of the realms of the too strange; and to craggy mountain or pastoral plain, overwhelming awe or calm social love, the poet reacted with suitable and explicit words of emotion.

A possible attitude toward this poetry and its vocabulary might be stated this way: These snatches represent not the best work of the best poets of the century, but the mean level of eighteenth-century faults. One of the worst faults is the false emotionalism, the elaborate statement glossing over a lack of real feeling. The presence of names does not signify the presence of felt meanings. The gulf between these men and Wordsworth in sincerity and skill is so great that no mere likeness in word or phrase or abun-

---

[43] *Ibid.,* XVI:173.
[44] *Ibid.,* XVI:70.

dance of these could have any meaning so far as the technique of poetry was concerned. In dealing with the vocabulary of feeling in the eighteenth century, however considerable it may be in amount, one is dealing with hollow shells.

But an attitude seems preferable which does not thus immediately call in doubt the value of so large a part of a century's poetry. *Sincerity,* for example, is a tricky word. Given a multitude of poets, the minor ones in general agreement with the major, all steadfastly and abundantly employing in their poetry a certain material of language, there seems more warrant for relating such usage to the theory of poetry behind it than for calling it unpoetic by one's own standards. To picture so many men loading their work with a material for which they did not greatly care is to be unfriendly to the craft of poetry as well as to the eighteenth century. To say with perfect friendliness, on the other hand, that the age was superb in its way, but that the way was one of prose and reason, is tyrannically to limit poetry by assuming that it is not a craft at all, but a special state of mind. If the Augustan champions of reason, thought, and wit had chosen to write their couplets without any literal expression of emotion, they might still have been setting down deeply emotional thinking; since that was not in fact their method, since their statement was literal, does that conversely mean it was unemotional? We must distinguish between human emotion and poetic conveyance of it.

Whatever a man's concern or a period's concern with science, logic, argument, satire, one would have to be a fairly bad psychologist to deny to that individual or society as much "sincere" and intrinsic emotional feeling as any other's. The difference would appear, rather than in depth of emotion, in methods of expression of the feeling and in the changing centers and associations of interest which condition those methods. Such a difference is visible between the eighteenth century and ballad literature, or between the eighteenth century and our own day. Many of the balladmakers and many of our contemporaries express the emotion in their poems exactly by not naming it, by making it implicit in sound and sense; this is possible for them partly because of the atmosphere of thought which did not in their time and does not now associate deep emotion with the names of emotion, but rather associates it with certain kinds of words and meanings which are of especial significance to the time and thus able to carry the weight in the poem.

In the eighteenth century, emotion and its names were closely equivalent in intensity, so that the very names could carry the strength of the emotion to the satisfaction of poets. One of the centers of experience to which feeling was most closely bound was that center which comprised the feelings themselves: they were of intellectual and emotional interest, major factors from society through cosmology, and of consequent importance to poetry. Therefore I find myself puzzled by the many critics who have commented to the effect that while the words of feeling in the eighteenth-century poetry might be the language of passion, they were not passion's language. I am under the impression that passion's language is as changing as the men who speak it, and that its changes are traceable. Nor can I see why any absolute prescription should make emotion stated less emotional. Mr. Utter in his discussion of the sentimental novel has suggested that "emotion by rule is insincerity, and insincerity of emotion is of the essence of sentimentality."[45] But rules grow out of interests and desires, as they particularly might have for the novel with few precedents; and if by "emotion by rule" Mr. Utter meant simply thoughtless imitation of strong writing, by second-raters, he was not unfair to the second-raters, but there should be no inference that the vast amount of eighteenth-century emotion was all second-rate.

I think the critics of the past century have been slighting eight-

---

[45] *Pamela's Daughters*, p. 102.

eenth-century emotion because of two particular biases of their own. When in the nineteenth century that interesting poetic technique began which desired the feeling to rise from the shadow of the poem, not from its surface, the technique perhaps reflected directly a new way of thought. At any rate, we had for a long time the feeling that the deepest emotion could only be implied, that it lay in the auras of objects and events, red roses across the moon, or the feet of Atalanta. By such a standard, Augustan poetry was indeed prose. Now again, from Richards and Eastman and their respective schools of complex association and vivid sense impression, we have an omission of the eighteenth century from poetry, still on the grounds of too explicit statement, of language "flat" and abstract, of a "philosophical" purpose. As attitudes, such critical divisions are illuminating, but as purportedly definitional they are unfortunate in tending, as they have so long done, to limit the very field of discussion and observation. This study, and perhaps a growing present liking for some eighteenth-century skills, arise respectively out of pleasure in detail for itself and pleasure in some particular details. We can be admittedly biased to advantage.

But one will say, Much of the stuff, the statement of emotion, already quoted as illustrative of the background for Wordsworth's emphasis seems definitely excessive, awkward, and bad. Does one tolerate it simply because it is present? In one way, yes, as it is indicative of eighteenth-century values; in one way, no, as it is foreign to our own general or individual values; in one way, both, by a temporary suspension of judgment. Granting poetry the material, one can observe by comparison how the material is used for better or worse, what its main forms and aspects are and how they change, and in what poets it appears to take on the glow of good treatment. Mr. Van Doren has suggested that, in the time of Dryden, theory and practice had not come together; that men wanted to write about passion passionately but were not practiced in that technique.[46] Mr. Draper has made the very interesting statement that

... generations of endeavor were needed to bridge the gulf between the crude emotionalism of a Puritan minister bewailing a deceased colleague and the lofty beauty of Shelley's *Adonais:* many lessons of culture had to be learned, and much of Classical restraint.... In the opinion of the present author, this advance in technical subtlety of emotional expression is perhaps the most important aspect of eighteenth century literature.[47]

These seem to me wise generalizations about a subject that requires in detail a great deal more knowledge than we have; to illustrate their truth in the material itself is a kind of process that requires both observation and personal reaction. The judgment of skill must still be colored somewhat by one's own values, but at least it works in terms of the poet's own choice.

The Pattern of the Material

From climate of opinion, then, one turns to texture of specific material: from the wide and firmly compacted philosophical background and conditioning setting of the eighteenth century to its poetic substance. Such concentrating entails a shift from quotation to a tabulation (table 2) showing, with greater precision, amounts and kinds. I hope it does not look pretentious or mathematical; it is supposed simply to be convenient. It is supposed to indicate in small space a little of the quantitative relationship obtaining in the vocabulary of feeling between some of the eighteenth-century poets, and between these and Wordsworth. It should make clear a major point: that from Pope to Wordsworth there was a continuity of interest and poetic expression of that interest, a group of words and their patterns which comprised a regular part of the substance of poetry.

[46] *The Poetry of John Dryden*, pp. 56–61. Note also p. 336; Van Doren warns those who write out of their nerves to beware their judgment of those who wrote out of their faculties.

[47] *The Funeral Elegy and the Rise of English Romanticism*, p. 326 and footnote.

In the first place, stated feeling, whether in complete long poems like Pope's, Johnson's, Goldsmith's, in parts of long poems like Armstrong's, Beattie's, Cowper's, or in collected pieces like Gray's, Collins', and the first two hundred pages of Dodsley, occurs at the least once in seven lines, mainly one in five, six, or seven, which is exactly Wordsworth's average. The exceptions, and these are on the side of larger amount, are the once in four lines of Gray and Collins, and the once in two of Pope's *Eloisa,* and the once in three of Armstrong on the passions, a work serving here as an example of direct didactic handling of the subject. In no sustained work did Wordsworth achieve the lavishness of one statement in four lines, except in his early *Guilt and Sorrow,* which suggests, since the themes are of the same variety, perhaps an early enthusiasm of the *Eloisa* school, a hardy variety indeed. On the whole, the variation between once in four, five, six, or seven lines which occurs both in Wordsworth and his predecessors is not one to be pressed. Though in the contrast between four and seven, between Gray and Johnson, there is a fair enough point, nevertheless, when one considers that the average of Eliot's *Waste Land* is one statement in twenty-five lines, one sees in the range from Pope to Wordsworth a relatively strong unanimity.

Second, and very important though not chartable, is the fact that no single poem of all those observed does without statement of emotion. Even the shortest poems of the Dodsley Miscellany, and of Gray and Collins, make use of statement. In the wider range of Wordsworth's poetry, on the other hand, there are some few that omit the names of feelings. None of them is notable as poetry, however, and the proportion is so small—a fraction of 1 per cent—that since our eighteenth-century samples are not so large and do not provide room for such minor variation, these few poems are of more interest in the minute study of Wordsworth himself than as any contrast to the eighteenth century. It may fairly be said, then, in generalization, that it was the habit of all these poets to state emotion as part of any subject, theme, and form they might choose to employ.

Third, there is the forwardness of the statement, its presence by vigor, point, elaboration, or structure, in the foreground of the poem. This matter is a somewhat subjective one: no two people would select all the same phrases as outstanding; on the other hand, the proportions as a whole are objective by the very fact that the distance between a notable statement and a passing reference is regularly great. The distinction depends of course upon context: *weeping* among a number of phrases vividly setting forth the weeping may be a pale background word, whereas by itself it may have an immense power. The importance of the distinction is simply that it makes clear different textures of usage. A poet may follow one elaborate phrase with another and another, so that his poem is solid with them; such a poem is *Eloisa to Abelard,* and its relatively high 40 per cent of elaborated statements represents this fact. Or the poet may move in so level a tone that even a very little device will make the phrase outstanding: as for example the stress of balance and contrast in Johnson's *Vanity of Human Wishes,* wherein emphatic phrasing amounts to 50 per cent of the total naming of emotion. Or, on the other hand, the poet may keep to that undistinguished pace for which Wordsworth and Cowper are notable, moving once in a while from everyday commonplace to an intensification of it; and for such poetry the percentage is less.

The figures in this matter represent a particularly interesting shift from the eighteenth century to Wordsworth, from the good writing of Pope, Johnson, Goldsmith, and Beattie, and, for that matter, the early Wordsworth, with its emphatic devices either of structure such as balance and contrast, or of figure, heavy and full-blown, to the thinner and paler quality of Collins, Cowper, and Wordsworth.[48] The nature of both the heroic couplet and

[48] Armstrong and Dodsley's are in this regard not representative of a style.

the Miltonian sublime blank verse fostered emphasis from phrase to phrase and image to piled-up image; when this tension lessened, often for long spaces, there was a laxer phrasing, a mild motion through the commonplace, or an absorbed satisfaction with the simple names and metaphors. The simple fact is that in the treatment of Wordsworth's vocabulary of emotion one can assume the general regularity and likeness and unembellishment of about three-fourths of it, this at intervals serving, without violent alteration, the increased intensity of the other fourth; while eighteenth-century poets in the Augustan tradition, as one is constantly reminded by the pressure of the figures, maintained twice as much stress of statement. One may call this, as it has been called, a false inflation; it was, at any rate, a consistent and earnest technique, and it may reflect again the purposeful attitude of poets toward their material of passion. By device they made it as constantly vivid as possible; for Wordsworth it was meaningful and poetic even in its plainest names. This is perhaps, then, a factor in that development of the poetic technique of handling feeling to which Mr. Draper made reference. With a changing general poetic style on the one hand and a growing familiarity with the meanings and associations of the names of emotions on the other, elaboration for the sake of significance became less needful, and some of Wordsworth's predecessors, though notably not Beattie and Crabbe, allowed the meaning to rest where it was collecting, in the simple terms. That the fanciest figures of Pope and his fellows were not abandoned, but used to advantage in muted or concentrated form, is evident in the material which next concerns us.

Fourth, the divisions of the noteworthy material into general statement, physical location, and so forth, as we saw in the first section, represent clear varieties of use—clear, that is, in Wordsworth's poetry. They are applied to the others, too, for the sake of comparison, not out of any illusion that they are the only fundamental divisions. In Wordsworth, such general abstract phrasing as "the longing for confirmed tranquillity" or "voluptuous unconcern" has a great vitality; has it also in the eighteenth century, and for the same qualities? Equally important to Wordsworth was the physical property of his emotion, the "felt in the blood and felt along the heart" phrasing. These two kinds amount to two-thirds of the notable material; the other third consists of three other types of use in almost equal proportions: that which bestows the feeling upon natural objects; that which gives sometimes human form, but usually simply some human attribute or external force to the emotion, as "Hope's perpetual breath"; and finally, that kind of association with a clearly distinct object which is often called metaphysical, and which should not here imply necessarily the far-fetched, but merely some sense of two units, as in "a heart, the fountain of sweet tears."

Are the proportions of these varieties of statement deeply different from Wordsworth's in the eighteenth century? Do the divisions natural to Wordsworth seem Procrustean for his predecessors? Under the general agreement respecting amount is there a basic disagreement respecting kind? Apparently not; apparently the Wordsworthian alliances are strong on detail.

Look first at general statement: in the major poets its range is from a third to a half; the poets of Dodsley's, Goldsmith, Johnson, Cowper, Wordsworth, agree closely; Pope's emphasis is somewhat heavier. In Armstrong's work, since it is a special problem, one may expect less philosophical generalization. Gray and Collins, then, are a little apart from the main line. Beneath the surface of the numbers is the quality of the writing itself. Pope's general phrases have, of course, their life only in their context, but even out of it they are warm: "Dim and remote the joys of saints I see," "Who seek in love for aught but love alone," "(O pious fraud of am'rous charity!),""Oh curst dear horrors of all-conscious night," "In sad similitude of griefs to mine," "A cool suspense from pleasure and from pain"—these from *Eloisa to Abelard;* and from the

Essay on Man: "Chaos of Thought and Passion, all confus'd," "Mere curious pleasure, or ingenious pain," "The joy, the peace, the glory of Mankind," "Each home-felt joy that life inherits here," and, for Pope's own triumphant conclusion,

> That *Reason, Passion,* answer one great aim;
> That true *Self-love* and *Social* are the same;
> That *Virtue* only makes our bliss below;
> And all our Knowledge is, *Ourselves to Know.*

Such phrasing seems to me to indicate a talent already matured in the handling of feeling as explicit material, in the generalizing about feeling out of a familiarity with its general relationships. As one must not forget, it was not that the naming of emotions or the elaboration of them had not been done or overdone in the Renaissance: the whole connection of Elizabethan to seventeenth-century technique is its own problem for discussion. It was simply that the late seventeenth-century predecessors of Pope were faced with new scientific material, new aesthetic material, and a gradually shaping new universal structure, with passions basic to the structure; and it is therefore remarkable that so soon as Pope the intellectual capacity for possessing the meaning of the relationships of sense, emotion, and thought had translated itself with such sensitiveness into the compression of poetry. It is of course true that selection lends advantage to our eyes, that the *Eloisa* average of one in two lines portends a thickness, and the theme of the *Essay on Man,* on the state of man in relation to society, happiness, and so on, a didacticism to which we should object. But a good deal of that comes from a different intention and theory of poetry and perhaps from some lack of experience in the practice of the theory, or rather an extra enthusiasm for all its possibilities. At any rate, both in context and in separation a great deal of Pope's emotional material seems to me to have a force and dexterity which by critics it has been earnestly denied.

In the Dodsley poems and Armstrong's chapter there is a less amount of concise or skillful general statement, but no actual lack of it. A common device is that of the list, the string of feelings; it is a favorite of Wordsworth, too.

> But fruitless, hopeless, disappointed, rack'd
> With jealousy, fatigued with hope and fear, ...

is one of Armstrong's, and from Arbuthnot's *Know Your Self* in Dodsley's,

> Thy lust, thy curiousity, thy pride,
> Curb'd or deferr'd, or balk'd, or gratify'd ...

The same sort of phrasing in Wordsworth's "Beloved Vale" (a lyric of the 1801–1807 period, the period which I am using as a basis for comparison here because it is typical in each proportion to his work as a whole), suggests with startling precision the lightened atmosphere which Wordsworth characteristically gave at best to eighteenth-century devices:

> I looked, I stared, I smiled, I laughed; and all
> The weight of sadness was in wonder lost.

But in his earlier *Guilt and Sorrow* Wordsworth too had his "Disease and famine, agony and fear," and in *Tintern Abbey,* "An appetite; a feeling and a love," and this very development of his technique is closely bound to the eighteenth century.

In most of the general statement from the poets of Dodsley's to Cowper no particular change in quality or variety is visible, except for this: that more of Pope's vividness of psychology appeared in Dodsley's than later: "the soft submissive fear," "the active lunacy of pride," "our joys are short and broken," while the force of Johnson and Goldsmith seems more in the balance and neatness than in the psychology: "With cheerful wisdom and instinctive mirth," "The sad historian of the pensive plain," and, as a notable example of structure in Goldsmith, "Return'd and wept, and still returned to weep."

Gray and Collins did not contribute new material in this field; they wrote in it as if it were natural to them, but not of such deep interest that their generalizations rose from the level of thorough and fairly elaborate material which Beattie and Cowper also employed. There seemed, in other words, to be a solid fund of main points and of variations upon these, not necessarily mechanical, but considered simply as good poetic material, allowing for much originality, for both the range in time from Pope to Wordsworth and the range in elaboration from Dodsley's, say, to Johnson. Gray and Collins, for all their pictorial tendencies, wrote such general description as "Now drooping, woeful wan, like one forlorn," and "Silent and pale, in wild amazement hung"; and in the contrast between these and Cowper's "His wrath is busy and his frown is felt" one notes still the old contrast between the tempered and the sublime styles, both of which were important to Pope.

All this material is in its nature absorbing for itself and for its reflection of the ways of thought of those who used it. It is not fairly compressible into the forms of illustration unless one devotes oneself for a whole study to a single phase. The perhaps arbitrary sound of some of my generalizations, then, is not to be avoided; the statements can do little more than imply the wealth of illustration.

Turning to the other aspects of the material, we find that they represent various shades of relationship. The location of feeling in the body, in the heart, the chill and burning, the fever of the breast, and so forth, which from eighteenth-century philosophy one would expect to be a fairly regular element, is so indeed; the only exceptions are Armstrong's larger amount, understandable because of his specific subject, and Gray's smaller amount, for which in my present knowledge of Gray I have no explanation. Wordsworth in this respect is in accord with most of his predecessors. On the other hand, in the bestowal of feeling upon natural objects he is in far closer relation to the poets who commonly bear the title of Pre-Romantics than to the others. This is exactly what one might expect from the generalizations long heard; it is evident that a changing attitude toward nature was part of the trend as it has been traced and that, as far as amount goes, Wordsworth preserved the trend but did not increase it. It is interesting to see as early as Pope's *Essay on Man* so delicate a passage of detailed feeling as its lines on the finer senses than man's, the feel of the spider along the line. In personification, even in its widest aspect as separable power, it is surprising to see Wordsworth on neither side of the clearest opposition, that between Johnson and Gray, but rather to find these along with Goldsmith and Collins in agreement upon strong use, with Wordsworth, Cowper, and the earlier Augustans slighting the device. And finally, this latter alliance appears even more strongly when, in the use of objectification, of all the poets Wordsworth is second to Dodsley's. Objectification, even in its simplest form as I refer to it here, was decidedly in the seventeenth-century manner, and it is not surprising to find it in the poets of Dodsley's, who, though some of them were a half century later, were artistically conservative. But the fact that Wordsworth too was closer to this manner than any of his immediate predecessors suggests both an added richness of complexity in him and also the source of that complexity.

In sum, then, by these divisions which seem to be natural to one or another of the eighteenth-century poets as well as to Wordsworth, one sees bound in the single strand of the material of stated emotion a number of eighteenth-century divergences or differing emphases, and a merging of all but one of these in Wordsworth. All making emotion a strong poetic material, most of these men, except for Gray and Collins, were practiced in its most abstract terms and generalizations; all but, again, Gray were accustomed to thinking of it often in physical terms, both in the signs and shows and in the deeper tremors; none was so great a purist as Johnson or Goldsmith in the rejection of emotion in natural ob-

jects, but this bestowed emotion's greatest acceptance came with
the later poets, including Wordsworth; the divisions were about
equal in the visualizing of passions as independent powers, with
Wordsworth on the side of the Augustan tradition; and finally,
all but the Dodsley poets were wary of objectification, but Wordsworth was the least wary.

Gray and Collins stand out clearly as men of a special mind.
They, and all the others they serve here to represent, make plain
even in so small a field as that of stated emotion their interest in
the visual, the pictorial. What, from the established figures, one
would call the main line is that which thought and wrote in
terms of principles and processes. Wordsworth was part of that
line. The minds of Gray and Collins had a different way of working; they are part of a main line I have not traced. It has often
been said that the *Elegy in a Country Church-yard* was an epitome
of a good deal of eighteenth-century platitude, and clearly it is in
its major aspects; but in some of its minor variations on the theme
of feeling it is apart from all the poetry we have observed here
except that of Collins.

> Chill Penury repress'd their noble rage,
> And froze the genial currents of the soul.

There is a solid eighteenth-century sentence. But in the poem as
a whole the personified first half is developed to an untypical degree: "And Melancholy marked him for her own." "He gave to
Mis'ry all he had, a tear."

Therefore such a comment as the following seems curiously
inadequate: that "during the course of the eighteenth century,
fancy, imagination, and emotion successfully reasserted their
rights," and that as an example William Collins "considered su-
perstitions and the passions proper subjects for poetry."[49] Emotion
had no need to reassert its rights; it had need rather, perhaps, to
calm down about them; and Collins' own particular brand of

---

[49] Clarence C. Green, *Neo-Classic Theory of Tragedy in England during the Eighteenth
Century*, p. 233.

emotion is interesting not as assertion of a theme, but as special variation upon it. Different from the usual graphic and moral philosophizing upon happiness, pride, and fear, different from the everyday panting hearts and flashing eyes, are the beings of *The Passions, An Ode for Music,* "But thou, O Hope, with Eyes so fair," "Next Anger rush'd, his Eyes on Fire," "With woful measures wan Despair," "Love fram'd with Mirth, a gay fantastic Round." And like these are many of Gray's: "Sorrow's faded form," "blue-eyed Pleasures," "The bloom of young Desire and purple light of Love." Even in the far milder form that Johnson and Goldsmith gave them, as "faith panting for a happier seat" and "grey-beard mirth and smiling toil," the passions received no such outward shape from Wordsworth except on a few memorable occasions. On the whole, it seemed he rejected this eighteenth-century type with its Miltonic tang in favor of the philosophical-scientific tradition.[50]

This tradition, from the eighteenth century, was his emphatic interest, and two other phases he took with resultant enrichment: the objectification from the early material, the affection of nature from the later. Most of the poets whom we have observed put more of a stress on one or another of the single phases of stated feeling than did Wordsworth; his was a more even blending. Most of the poets agree thoroughly in the broader outlines of statement as a whole and some of its means; when they disagree, the disagreements appear to be parallel rather than consecutive in time, except in the reference to nature's feelings; and the resultant variations, with this one exception, create no trend.

One would conclude that the century was of a mind on the subject of passion, and that its schools of thought within that mind, with their varying interests in physiology, social ethics, strange-

---

[50] For an interesting discussion of this phase in Collins, cf. Bush, *op. cit.,* as, p. 21: "In keeping with this inflated Miltonese was the vogue of personified abstractions, which became notable about 1742 . . ."; and p. 34. Also Leavis, *Revaluations,* p. 108, on the fact that "fancy" is the Muse invoked by Collins when Milton was the inspiration. Consider Wordsworth's relative lack of interest in fancy.

ness and awe, visual excitement, universal structure, set up in poetry a constant interplay of devices for their own emphases, their own ideas of the effective and the poetic; and one would conclude that the result in poetry was a rich, to some tastes an overrich, texture of expression in language, constant, emphatic, and various, which comprised a substantial part of what in that century poetry had to say.

A mechanical support to the conclusion is the information supplied by the Concordances of Pope, Gray, and Wordsworth. Of the ten or a dozen words, apart from common connectives, most used by these three at respectively the beginning, the middle, and the turn of the century two or three are surpassingly large in number. In Pope these are *man, see,* and *love;* in Gray they are *see, eye,* and *love;* in Wordsworth, *see, love, life, man.* If to elaborate upon these bare facts would not seem so fanciful, I should enjoy pointing out how decisively they uphold some of the surmises of this study: first, that a major concern of the three was emotion; second, that while Gray's was the envisioned or imaged scene, Wordsworth's and Pope's was more generalized emotion. But this may be considered abstraction carried to Words worth's point: its similarity to imagination.

"Emotion" and "Romantic"

Emotion is not, at any rate, a term to use in the defining of Wordsworth's poetry, or his period's poetry, or "Romantic" poetry set over against the poetry of the eighteenth century. Emotion is rather the material of a bond. When one asks if Wordsworth and his contemporaries characteristically revived emotion, the answer is "Yes" only if one is speaking in terms of a personal valuation of effect or arbitrary definition of emotion; otherwise the substance of a hundred and fifty years of poetry speaks for itself in its own names of *love, fear, hope, pleasure.* For that matter, more than a hundred and fifty years' use of the term *romantic* speaks

for itself to the same effect. *Romantic* in its own day had no definitional connection with *emotion*. Irving Babbitt in summarizing
its meaning suggested,

> In general a thing is romantic when, as Aristotle would say, it is
> wonderful rather than probable; in other words, when it violates the
> normal sequence of cause and effect in favor of adventure.... A thing
> is romantic when it is strange, unexpected, intense, superlative, ex-
> treme, unique, etc. A thing is classical, on the other hand, when it is
> not unique, but representative of a class.[51]

Fulke-Greville first used the word, in 1628, according to the Oxford Dictionary, and not until two centuries later, in 1851, was
reference made by it to "that new school of literature." In the
interval, *romantic* was used with consistent clarity. Henry More,
1659, "I speak especially of that Imagination which is most free,
such as we use in Romantick Inventions." Pepys, 1667, "almost
romantique, and yet true." Addison, *Italy,* 1705, "It is so Romantic
a Scene that it has always probably given occasion to such Chi-
merical Relations." Hurd, Letter III, 1762, "What may truly be
called romantic, the going in quest of adventures." And Johnson's
Dictionary, "Romantic: (1) Resembling the tales of romances:
wild; (2) Improbable; false; (3) Fanciful; full of wild scenery.

It is not always that a word fits its range of meaning as tightly
as this one does; but it had later to take over a later century's
meanings. Even now in its colloquial sense it is nearer perhaps
to Dr. Johnson's summations than to others, and that prevailing
sense is one that we have seen to be very important to eighteenth-
century theory. The realm of the romantic: it is the realm of
the sublime, the mountainous, the thrilling, the terrifying, the
strange: it is one half of that aesthetic which kept dividing into
the sublime and the pathetic, or the beautiful as Burke defined

---

[51] *Rousseau and Romanticism*, p. 4. And see A. O. Lovejoy, *Mod. Lang. Notes*, XLII:
450, for a thorough discussion of the uses of the term, with lists and bibliography.
Also *PMLA*, XXXIX:229–253. The suggestion made by George Mead, *Movements of
Thought—the Nineteenth Century,* and others, concerning the romantic consciousness of
self-plus-object needs close study.

it; into the strange and the natural, both of which were bound to the feelings. It led into that technique of landscape, of personification, of visualization, which was of major importance to those poets of whom Gray and Collins were representative. In his use of many of its themes and devices Wordsworth too was "romantic," and in his rejection of the startling he was an opponent. But his emotion and his use of it were of a realm which underlay both the romantic and its opposite, which contained all the interweaving tendencies, and so, but for his special blendings, emotion and its use had been for at least a century before him. "Romantic" was one kind of modification for "emotion." Wordsworth used it as an adjective with *dreams, days, Spain, joy, sorrows, interest, hope;* he literally used it as a limiting term for emotions.

As such, there remains much still to be learned about it. The course of stated romantic emotion is a course in which Pope, Gray, Wordsworth all had part, but it was for them on the whole, or for Pope and Wordsworth at least, a minor course. Strange, intense, superlative, extreme, unique emotions were not the major concern of poets who would set forth the universal likenesses in men. Subtly personal and complex emotions, as they came to be better and better phrased in poetry, owed much to Wordsworth's example in skill and sensitivity, but little to his intention. For with part of the eighteenth century before him he was a poet of the general, the standard, the natural in its representative sense, and he had use for personal foibles or extremes no more in the heart than in landscape or society. To the degree that his perceptions and associations did indeed deviate from the accepted standard, in his emotional response to flowers and situations unresponded to before him, his critics might have called his emotion romantic. But since they considered it lowly rather than uplifting, exciting, or intense, they called it for a while merely idiosyncratic.

There is place then for discussion of emotion as romantic, but Wordsworth holds only a tentative and tenuous position in that place. While a more elaborate vocabulary of emotion flashed about him in true romantic fashion, he was demonstrating the delicate relations to sense, to thing, to individual feeling which vocabulary could possess. But his purpose was a generalizing, not a particularizing or complicating purpose, and the resulting material was in continuity with eighteenth-century material. Whatever the breaks between 1700 and 1800, the vocabulary of emotion was in part a bond.

IV. THE MATERIAL OF EMOTION
AND INDIVIDUAL SKILL:
WORDSWORTH

EARLY PRACTICE

W HEN, "anno aetatis 14," Wordsworth at Hawkshead wrote a school exercise in couplets, most heroic, he was confronted with proper poetic material at its most proper and accepted level, of age about a century, of range from laureates' celebrations to those by the companions at Hawkshead. And included in this material there seems to have been a good amount of the passions, for into these Wordsworth launched with alacrity and a zest that shows itself in the phrasing.

> While thus I mused, methought, before mine eyes,
> The Power of EDUCATION seemed to rise;
> Not she whose rigid precepts trained the boy
> Dead to the sense of every finer joy;
> Nor that vile wretch who bade the tender age
> Spurn Reason's law and humour Passion's rage;
> But she who trains the generous British youth
> In the bright paths of fair majestic Truth:
> ... Close at her side were all the powers, designed
> To curb, exalt, reform the tender mind:
> With panting breast, now pale as winter snows,
> Now flushed as Hebe, Emulation rose;
> ... I gazed upon the visionary train,
> Threw back my eyes, returned, and gazed again.
> When lo! the heavenly goddess thus began,
> Through all my frame the pleasing accents ran.

Apart from the fact, on the one hand, that such lines speak to value-standards and meaning-associations different from ours, and apart from the fact, on the other, that they were created more by a tradition than by Wordsworth, there is nothing very blameworthy about them. They are simple, standard expressions of a way of thought and a consequent way of poetry. In Pope, they would have far greater individuality, deftness, shine; but even in the school exercise they have at least life, as: "And lulled the warring passions into rest," "With mazy rules perplex the weary mind," "No longer steel their indurated hearts," "When Virtue weeps in agony of woe,"

> Do thou, if gratitude inspire thy breast,
> Spurn the soft fetters of lethargic rest.

These phrasings are mainly of two kinds, physical location and personification, and this is not a mixture characteristic of any single predecessor, but one seemingly drawn from the Gray manner on one side and the Augustan manner on the other. It seems hardly a clever fusion, for this reason: that the very presence of so much abstract personification of feeling tends to vitiate the equally large amount of physical feeling, however vividly expressed. The trains of personages can have little to do in the same field with the beating of the heart, the immediate sensation is forced to leap to the monumental figure, and there is neither perspicuous generalization nor startling conceit to tie the two. The devices of feeling in the Hawkshead poem, then, though both vivid and abundant, every four lines, reveal little sense of felt connection, and the poem to a discerning judge in any era would justly seem stagnant, as school exercises are expected to be. Nevertheless, Wordsworth knew what he thought was necessary to the poem, and put the feeling in with a will.

He knew, too, almost as early, that such feeling was important to him, for in the brief poem "Written in Very Early Youth," a sensitive and personal lyric, he contrives to speak it more individually. This is the atmosphere of poetry for the young poet:

> Calm is all nature as a resting wheel.
> The kine are couched upon the dewy grass;
> The horse alone, seen dimly as I pass,
> Is cropping audibly his later meal:
> Dark is the ground; a slumber seems to steal
> O'er vale and mountain, and the starless sky.

> Now, in this blank of things, a harmony,
> Home-felt, and home-created, comes to heal
> That grief for which the senses still supply
> Fresh food; for only then, when memory
> Is hushed, am I at rest. My Friends! restrain
> Those busy cares that would allay my pain;
> Oh! leave me to myself, nor let me feel
> The officious touch that makes me droop again.

Again the methods were a little mixed, the figure not consistent with itself, I think, yet in the atmosphere that Wordsworth provided there was at least a surface blend.

But now in the next few years he was reading more poetry, and growing fond of words. It was not now merely the passages of Spenser, Shakespeare, Milton which his father had him memorize, nor merely the Pope and Gray he used consciously as models;[1] it was now Ovid and the various poets he referred to in his notes to the "Evening Walk," notably Thomson. Poetry was now scene, variety, and above all, image.

> And, fronting the bright west, yon oak entwines
> Its darkening boughs and leaves, in stronger lines.

This is feebly and imperfectly expressed [said Wordsworth, looking back upon the poem], but I recollect distinctly the very spot where this first struck me. It was in the way between Hawskhead and Ambleside, and gave me extreme pleasure. The moment was important in my poetical history; for I date from it my consciousness of the infinite variety of natural appearances which had been unnoticed by the poets of any age or country, so far as I was acquainted with them; and I made a resolution to supply in some degree, the deficiency. I could not have been at that time above fourteen years of age. The description of the swans that follows, was taken from the daily opportunities I had of observing their habits, . . .

This famous passage on an interest basic to Wordsworth, appended as it was to "An Evening Walk," applied to topics like

---

[1] See Emile Legouis, *The Early Life of William Wordsworth*, trans. Matthews, pp. 38, 121, 124, for Wordsworth's reading. He notes (p. 127) the background of Pope and Goldsmith for the Hawkshead poem, and it is interesting to see in the material of feeling how without fusion the two are used. Note also De Quincey's description of Wordsworth and a companion skating and "chanting, with one voice, the verses of Goldsmith and of Gray." *Literary Reminiscences* (Boston, 1854), p. 316.

these, as he listed them: Moonlight, Hope, Night-sounds, Conclusion, and to lines like these:

> In youth's keen eye the livelong day was bright,
> The sun at morning, and the stars at night,
> Alike, when first the bittern's hollow bill
> Was heard, or woodcocks roamed the moonlight hill.
> In thoughtless gaiety I coursed the plain,
> And hope itself was all I knew of pain;
> For then, the inexperienced heart would beat
> At times, while young Content forsook her seat,
> And wild Impatience, pointing upward, showed,
> Through Passes yet unreached, a brighter road.[2]

The sun at morning and the stars at night, in other words, still were not satisfying without the explicit beating of the heart, and that itself leaped into figures of Content's seat, and the wildness of Impatience. Though in such lines the associations seem a little stiff, Wordsworth was capable in the same poem of combining the "infinite variety of natural appearances" with feeling images smoothly and firmly:

> Last evening sight, the cottage smoke, no more,
> Lost in the thickened darkness, glimmers hoar;
> And, towering from the sullen dark-brown mere,
> Like a black wall, the mountain-steeps appear.
> —Now o'er the soothed accordant heart we feel
> A sympathetic twilight slowly steal,
> And ever, as we fondly muse, we find
> The soft gloom deepening on the tranquil mind.

It would seem that his increasing interest in the describing of natural objects somewhat tempered Wordsworth's treatment of feeling, making it more psychological in terms of the subject

---

[2] I have used consistently Wordsworth's own revised version of all the poetry, as printed in the standard editions. The original versions of the "Evening Walk" and the "Descriptive Sketches" are quite different from the revised, but I have not made an exception of them, since the material of emotion was not so changed as to alter total proportions or types. The major revision in this material was the toning down and better assimilating of personification. A closer comparison of the versions would make an interesting study in itself, as much for what Wordsworth retained as for what he altered. Such comparison is now made even more profitable by the new De Selincourt edition of the *Works*, which was not available at the time of my study, though the *Letters* fortunately were.

matter, less extreme in terms of standard expression. It must be remembered that all quotations here used are illustrative, not singular, and that the generalizations about development of style that can be made are made not by single passages but by sums.

Consider, then, the sums.[3] We have seen that the emotion terms of the "Exercise" were vividly physical or personified but without much blend. The other types were relatively characterless. In "An Evening Walk," which uses statement less, once in seven lines, the statements are more evenly varied. There are a few good generalizations such as "How graceful pride can be, and how majestic, ease," which in its structure suggests its background; and there are one or two hints of conceit, as the twilight on the heart. Further, as one might expect from the increasing influence of the descriptive poets, there are some bestowals of feeling upon nature, especially in the scene of the swans. There is a good deal, then, in spite of persisting and pleasant personification, of the associated moods of nature and heart later to be characteristic of Wordsworth's poetry. And a quality of these moods, their generality, is not only noticeable in this early poem, but expressly commented on in the note to it regarding natural objects:

> I will conclude my notice of this poem by observing that the plan of it has not been confined to a particular walk or an individual place,— a proof (of which I was unconscious at the time) of my unwillingness to submit the poetic spirit to the chains of fact and real circumstance. The country is idealized rather than described in any one of its local aspects.

Too many quotations of the oak episode and the "infinite variety of natural appearances" omit this conclusion, which has an equal authenticity of attitude and alters immeasurably the significance of Wordsworth's interest in nature here, an interest which had already taken a step toward the developed theory of the prefaces, though "unconscious at the time." So the generalizing "the" of the eighteenth century is strongly in evidence, "the soothed ac-

---

[3] See table 1, page 169, for organized detail, as continuing basis for statement.

cordant heart," "the tranquil mind"; and it is possible to note
with distinction that "sighs will ever trouble human breath."

Although the "Descriptive Sketches" are usually considered
along with "An Evening Walk," the two having been written
close together and published together in 1793, there are interesting differences within the material of emotion. The earlier poem
seemed to be working toward a personal blending of elements:
the Sketches seem much more literary and extreme.' For example,
the bodily location of emotion, which was strong through the
eighteenth century is strong here also, amounting to almost one-
half, and the expressions are clearly eighteenth-century, as "Soft
bosoms breathe around contagious sighs," "And watered duly
with the pious tear," "Soon with despair's whole weight his spirits
sink," and so forth. That Wordsworth could employ the device
with his own capable invention is indicated by such variations
as "Rouses the soul from her severe delight," "Awoke a fainter
sense of moral grief," and, hauntingly, "And thou, lost fragrance
of the heart, return!" But the large amount of traditional phraseology suggests a preoccupation with tradition, and the whole
pattern of the poem, the general survey type, like Goldsmith's
"Traveller," substantiates this suggestion of preoccupation. The
lack in this version of the pattern was Wordsworth's own: that
is, a lack of strong general philosophical statement. Of both personification and bestowal there are many solid passages; again,
one sees, a combination of materials; and the one contribution
new to Wordsworth's skill so far is the increase and noteworthi-
ness of objectifying images, as remarkably in this passage:

> The mind condemned, without reprieve, to go
> O'er life's long deserts with its charge of woe,
> With sad congratulation joins the train
> Where beasts and men together o'er the plain
> Move on—a mighty caravan of pain:

' Note the contrast between Legouis's epithets for the *Sketches* style—"perverse," "distorted," "corrupt" (*op. cit.*, p. 123), and the descriptive phrase "a quite orthodox piece
of local verse" by Dwight Durling, in *The Georgic Tradition in English Poetry*, p. 212.

One surmises that this poem, and the "Female Vagrant," which is much like it in vocabulary of feeling, were written out of enthusiasm for reading, and that the reading had lately included something with a tang of the metaphysical, perhaps simply Pope, as the *Sketches* figure of the lark of hope, like Pope's, might suggest. At any rate, from the style of the "Evening Walk," which is relatively even and personal in the material of feeling and its connections, there is a shift to the more lurid and the more uneven, the suggestion of many styles, flashes of much skill and individuality, on the whole a play rather than a sobering philosophy of abstraction and of connection.

> To loathsome vaults where heart-sick anguish tossed,
> Hope died, and fear itself in agony was lost!

Such a couplet is not a fair example of the whole style of the "Female Vagrant"; there are much better passages within it; yet it is representative of an interest Wordsworth had in the early 'nineties in the words for their own glory, the piling of effects, the physical that was not subtly psychological. "The Female Vagrant" and, in its enlarged form, "Guilt and Sorrow" elaborate the literary devices about which the poet was eager, and, not having the simplicity of "An Evening Walk," have not the control of sights and sounds to sober them; have not, either, the force of much clear attitude to crystallize their assumed vocabulary in one shape or another.

To these, then, "The Borderers" of 1795 is in notable contrast. It possesses neither the Wordsworthian simplicity nor the imitative density. It uses statement somewhat more sparingly: half as often as "Guilt and Sorrow"; it has its own special nature, and that nature is one of assured good writing. The forthrightness and dash of its style suggests that in the brief space of two years or so its author had changed admirations and begun to make up his mind; the control is not the control of scenes and sentiments so wholly, but also of thought. Statistically the change is evident mainly in the increase of objectification, especially in the conceit form, to a fifth, and in the proportionate lessening of bestowal and personification; further than this, the abstractions, though no more abundant, make more sense. The characteristic quality of "The Borderers," thoughtful analysis, by means of metaphor, is not to be a major characteristic of any of Wordsworth's later work, but is to remain a minor one, and its sudden presence so fully in 1795 before any meeting with Coleridge, and Coleridge's happy acceptance of it complete, is significant. This is the way it sounds:

> ... I perceive
> That fear is like a cloak which old men huddle
> About their love, as if to keep it warm.

> ... His face bespeaks
> A deep and simple meekness: and that Soul,
> Which with the motion of a virtuous act
> Flashes a look of terror upon guilt,
> Is, after conflict, quiet as the ocean,
> By a miraculous finger, stilled at once.

> ... These fools of feeling are mere birds of winter
> That haunt some barren island of the north,
> Where, if a famishing man stretch forth his hand,
> They think it is to feed them.

> ... Rainbow arches
> Highways of dreaming passion, have too long
> Young as he is, diverted wish and hope
> From the unpretending ground we mortals tread;—

> ... Leave that thought awhile,
> As one of those beliefs, which in their hearts
> Lovers lock up as pearls, though oft no better
> Than feathers clinging to their points of passion.[5]

The very movement and structure of these sentences is so different from the usual early style of Wordsworth, and from his

[5] These five quotations from "The Borderers" are, respectively: I, ll. 21–23; I, ll. 168–173; II, ll. 8–11; II, ll. 380–383; IV, ll. 28–31.

style as a whole in their proportionate number, that one must wonder what lightning of thought had struck the poet. The sound is of Shakespeare; it is in a sense metaphysical, but not labored in the Donne degree; it has a ring smooth, elaborate, suggesting a wide and deep range of thought, and the blank verse has the sound of being spoken. The fact that "The Borderers" is a drama would indicate that Wordsworth had dramatic models, and the character of the stated emotion would indicate that one of the noblest of these was Shakespeare. We have seen in the earlier poems some few uses of the conceit, and they were good, but simpler and of a kind familiar easily to Pope. But the "Borderers" phrasing is, I think, not Popean; its delicacy, which was natural to Wordsworth, was now active in a richer and more pliable material. Consider the motion of speech in this passage: how sinews have been given to Remorse:

> It cannot live with thought; think on, think on,
> And it will die. What! in this universe,
> Where the least things control the greatest, where
> The faintest breath that breathes can move a world;
> What! feel remorse, where, if a cat had sneezed,
> A leaf had fallen, the thing had never been
> Whose very shadow gnaws us to the vitals.[6]

This is dramatic stuff not personal for Wordsworth, at least for the usual Wordsworth. His skill can play in this wider and less familiar area of mind.

I think, too, that the stimulus was not only exterior but interior, that Wordsworth was building up a pattern of thought to condition his usages. What makes this process plain is the preface to "The Borderers" which Professor de Selincourt has summarized.[7] In that prose Wordsworth for the first time set down his theoretical emphasis upon universal man, Man as type, passions

---

[6] "The Borderers," III, ll. 427–433.

[7] Ernest de Selincourt, "The Hitherto Unpublished Preface to 'The Borderers,' " *Nineteenth Century*, C:723–741. The reference to *Othello* in this preface supports the impression of immediate influence of Shakespearean style.

as fundamental themes. His interest, turning to character full and dramatic, took with it the implements to which it was already so accustomed, particularly the eighteenth-century phrasing of the psychology of feeling, and *man* and *passion* became his key critical words. Many years later, when "The Borderers" was published, he expressed, in terms of a settled attitude, dissatisfaction with much of the style, but content with its central success as a study of men's passions.[8]

This preoccupation which he had acquired by the middle of the 'nineties was visible in the increased power of abstract statement in "The Borderers." So far, that had been one of the eighteenth-century powers which Wordsworth had not lived up to; now, not only did the figured devices for stating emotion by personification and conceit and physical location take on intensity, but generalizations with the quality of definition also appeared and were vigorous. There was, for example, that memorable passage:

> Action is transitory—a step, a blow,
> The motion of a muscle—this way or that—
> 'Tis done, and in the after-vacancy
> We wonder at ourselves like men betrayed:
> Suffering is permanent, obscure and dark,
> And shares the nature of infinity.[9]

One sees added to the capabilities of the young poet's absorbed style of his more immediate predecessors the new element of the complex intellectual metaphor of an earlier day, and along with it a formulating abstract philosophy and expression of it. These are signal lines in Wordsworth's poetry:

> And you should see how deeply I could reason
> Of love in all its shapes, beginnings, ends;
> Of moral qualities in their diverse aspects;
> Of actions, and their laws and tendencies.[10]

[8] Wordsworth's own introductory note.
[9] III, ll. 405–410.   [10] III, ll. 90–93.

CRITICAL CONSCIOUSNESS

Nevertheless, within another three years, Wordsworth was renouncing many of his young means to this main end. He was fixing in the *Lyrical Ballads* and the "major work" of *The Recluse* a style different in general effect from these that had gone before, contrived by a new balancing of the elements of all of them. The simplest abstract statement was considerably increased, the physical was considerably decreased, the affections of nature were given a larger place, larger on the whole than that of personification and objectification together. The elaborations of device were fading before the self-sufficiency of the plain general words. If this was a simplification, it was also a flattening, without respect for the derogation in that so lately fashionable critical term. There were fewer pains, pangs, and pressures of the heart, fewer senses bound with stony horror, fewer flashes of the eye, and along with this subdual went a removal of a great number of capital letters signifying the presences of Hope and Fear in their dwelling places, and along with the lessened activity of these Beings went the lessened activity of objects not usually associated with emotion, as conceit became everyday metaphor. In the texture of the evolved material there was a consequent greater smoothness, the smoothing of edges, less "outstanding" phraseology, and a general atmosphere of interplay between man and nature as the simple terms of feeling concerned them both. This is the material we observed in the first section, from the *Lyrical Ballads,* and with this Wordsworth was consciously working for his larger poem.

For by the time of the Preface to the *Lyrical Ballads,* 1800, Wordsworth had some conscious policies about details of style. The third section of this study concerns itself with the philosophical background of these policies, the organization of thought whereby interest in the general human faculties and their relationship to experience conditioned specific material and language in poetry itself. Here we may note an example of the attitude in Wordsworth's explicit mention of personification, the device he had himself so recently employed with some good effect.

Except in a very few instances the Reader will find no personifications of abstract ideas in these volumes, not that I mean to censure such personifications: they may well be fitted for certain sorts of composition, but in these Poems I propose to my self to imitate, and, as far as possible, to adopt the very language of men, and I do not find that such personifications make any regular or natural part of that language. I wish to keep my Reader in the company of flesh and blood, persuaded that by so doing I shall interest him. Not but that I believe that others who pursue a different track may interest him likewise. I do not interfere with their claim, I only wish to prefer a different claim of my own.

By 1802 Wordsworth had become more emphatic and less tolerant. His revised Preface[11] mentioned in this paragraph no other claims, and provided for personifications in an added sentence:

... They are, indeed, a figure of speech occasionally prompted by passion, and I have made use of them as such, but I have endeavoured utterly to reject them as a mechanical device of style, or as a family language which writers in metre seem to lay claim to by prescription.

From the years immediately after the publication of the *Lyrical Ballads* come other specific comments on the changing means of expression, reflecting a settling theory. A letter of 1801, for example, casts a most interesting backward look upon the "Descriptive Sketches" and the "Evening Walk":

They are juvenile productions, inflated and obscure, but they contain many new images, and vigorous lines; and they would perhaps interest you, by shewing how very widely different my former opinions must have been from those which I hold at present.

... You flatter me, Madam, that my style is distinguished by a genuine simplicity. Whatever merit I may have in this way I have attained solely by endeavouring to look, as I have said in my preface, steadily

---

[11] For important differences between the version of 1800 and those of 1802 and 1805, see *The Lyrical Ballads, 1798–1805,* with introduction and notes by George Sampson (3d ed.; London, 1914).

at my subject. If you read over carefully the Poem of the Female Vagrant, which was the first written of the collection (indeed it was written several years before the others) you will see that I have not formerly been conscious of the importance of this rule. The diction of that Poem is often vicious, and the descriptions are often false, giving proofs of a mind inattentive to the true nature of the subject on which it was employed.[12]

The major changes suggested by such grim analysis are not actually evident in the material of feeling. That material had a substantiality with which Wordsworth had begun and grown up; the rejections he came to make within it were rejections of excessive device, but not of the traditional device as a whole. The *Lyrical Ballads* were more ascetic in this regard than any of the poems after them, but even they, as we have seen, did more of smoothing and subduing than of rejection, in the vocabulary of emotion. The reminiscence of the *Prelude* itself, in its section on Books, is mildly friendly toward the youthful enthusiasms, liking words "For their own *sakes,* a passion, and a power," even though "full oft the objects of our love Were false, and in their splendor over-wrought."

> ... In fine,
> I was a better judge of thoughts than words,
> Misled in estimating words, not only
> By common inexperience of youth,
> But by the trade in classic niceties,
> The dangerous craft, of culling term and phrase
> From languages that want the living voice
> To carry meaning to the natural heart;
> To tell us what is passion, what is truth,
> What reason, what simplicity and sense.[13]

Such is a just criticism of the unassociated phrases of the Hawkshead exercise and the ponderous phrases of "The Female Vagrant"; but by its reliance on *heart* and *passion* such criticism makes plain that it was satisfied at least with these words if not their phrases.

---

[12] *Early Letters,* p. 270.   [13] *Prelude,* VI, ll. 105–115.

In other passages of reminiscence the *Prelude* made additional criticism of the material of feeling in respect to some of its attitudes. It is curious, in a way, that the full-formed critical attitude of a poet toward his work should appear in the very second decade of that work, that we should pause after one handful of poems and after one major volume, the *Ballads,* to attend to stocktaking; but before 1807, the publication of the next major collection, the stock had been taken, in some of the formal prose which we have already observed, and in the philosophical poetry itself. Immediately following the vagaries of experiment, then, we have the comment upon those vagaries, and the conscious selection of permanent elements from them. Rejected, in addition to "splendid" phrases, were two main attitudes of feeling: the extramelancholic, and the extravivid or pictorial. It is clear that in a measure all these rejections are one, and that they account for the perceptible change in the material of feeling between the earlier work and the *Lyrical Ballads:* the lessening of the vivid physical, personified, and metaphoric; the increase of the general and the affections of nature.

Two eighteenth-century fashions of feeling, then, Wordsworth explicitly recognized as having himself participated in during his youth, and abandoned upon his formulation of his own principles. Both he states in the *Prelude* with skill and a certain sympathy. The melancholy:

> Moods melancholy, fits of spleen, that loved
> A pensive sky, sad days, and piping winds,
>
> ... To feed a Poet's tender melancholy
> And fond conceit of sadness,
>
> ... Dejection taken up for pleasure's sake,
> And gilded sympathies, the willow wreath,
> And sober posies of funereal flowers,
> Gathered among those solitudes sublime
> From formal gardens of the lady Sorrow,
> Did sweeten many a meditative hour.

> ... Yet still in me with those soft luxuries
> Mixed something of stern mood, an under-thirst
> Of vigour seldom utterly allayed:[14]

Such a figure as the garden of the lady Sorrow was, by the time he wrote it, rare in Wordsworth's vocabulary of emotion, yet in its association with the past he used it as if with fondness, and it was later to have more company in his poetry again, not less. Here is his whole description of that past style of his, which was not later to be so different a style as the tone of the description might imply:

> But when that first poetic faculty
> Of plain Imagination and severe,
> No longer a mute influence of the soul,
> Ventured at some rash Muse's earnest call,
> To try her strength among harmonious words;
> And to book-notions and the rules of art
> Did knowingly conform itself; there came
> Among the simple shapes of human life
> A wilfulness of fancy and conceit;
> And Nature and her objects beautified
> These fictions, as in some sort, in their turn,
> They burnished her. From touch of this new power
> Nothing was safe: the elder-tree that grew
> Beside the well-known charnel-house had then
> A dismal look: the yew-tree had its ghost,
> That took his station there for ornament:
> The dignities of plain occurrence then
> Were tasteless, and truth's golden mean, a point
> Where no sufficient pleasure could be found.
> Then, if a widow, staggering with the blow
> Of her distress, was known to have turned her steps
> To the cold grave in which her husband slept,
> One night, or haply more than one, through pain
> Or half-insensate impotence of mind,
> The fact was caught at greedily, and there
> She must be visitant the whole year through,
> Wetting the turf with never-ending tears.[15]

---

[14] *Prelude*, VI, ll. 173–174; 366–367; 551–559.
[15] VIII, ll. 365–390.

For a modern reader, such phrases might seem only too accurately to describe the whole body of Wordsworthian poetry: the yew kept on having its emotion, the widow kept returning to the grave, the ground stayed wet with tears. But for Wordsworth himself there was a discrimination in degree to be made. The material of feeling as a whole was natural as it filled his atmosphere out of the atmosphere of the eighteenth century; but in some of its excesses, as he at first used them, he came to see little good. His desire was to temper the material; and part of this desire was philosophical, part more specifically literary. In part it rose from his now formulated fundamental principles concerning the primacy of simple general human truth not exaggerated; in part, from his now practiced good sense about the sound and quality of meanings unforced by patterns foreign to them. The ideas and the language were settling down together. The tears of melancholy, though they did not vanish, ceased a flow unnecessary to the general point. The vivid emotions for which the Enthusiast had gone in search in the eighteenth century, and for which Wordsworth had lately gone in search through the same Alps and countrysides, ceased their trust in the eye which was the avenue to the heart and began to resent the eye's most startling images and the heart's consequent violent but shallow agitations.

The whole salvation of the hero of the *Prelude* lay in this latter rejection. The scorn of the easy melancholy came relatively early in the poem; the scorn of the thrilling came only after the crisis of the French Revolution had been related; the "conflict of sensations without name," when the flaw in the poet's modes of happiness had become apparent through much perturbation:

> Vivid the transport, vivid though not profound;
> I roamed from hill to hill, from rock to rock,
> Still craving combinations of new forms,
> New pleasure, wider empire for the sight,
> Proud of her own endowments, and rejoiced
> To lay the inner faculties asleep.

> ...I speak in recollection of a time
> When the bodily eye, in every stage of life
> The most despotic of our senses, gained
> Such strength in *me* as often held my mind
> In absolute dominion.[16]

In the final book of the *Prelude* the problem was resolved, and Dorothy was the resolver, calling the poet back from his search for excitement and a more satisfying system of thought to an "exquisite regard for common things."

> I too exclusively esteemed *that* love,
> And sought *that* beauty, which, as Milton sings,
> Hath terror in it. Thou didst soften down
> This over-sternness; but for thee, dear Friend!
> My soul, too reckless of mild grace, had stood
> In her original self too confident,
> Retained too long a countenance severe;
> A rock with torrents roaring, with the clouds
> Familiar, and a favourite of the stars;
> But thou didst plant its crevices with flowers,
> Hang it with shrubs that twinkle in the breeze,
> And teach the little birds to build their nests
> And warble in its chambers.[17]

So the problems of style for Wordsworth in his central period of creation and criticism reflected his problems of life. As looking back on his beginning work he found its phrasing sometimes too elaborate, so also looking at his youth he thought its interests too elaborate, and consequently, with his sister's aid and the aid of an increasingly simple philosophical pattern, he removed from life and work the inherited emphases on the melancholy, the pictorial, the terrible, those phases of the sublime which were characteristic of the Pre-Romantics. This is not to say that he gave up such material, but rather that he subdued it. Further, this is not to say that he was dissatisfied with his early work as a whole— at least what we have of it. He allowed "Guilt and Sorrow," the

---

[16] *Prelude*, XII, ll. 127–147.
[17] XIV, ll. 244–256.

elaborated "Female Vagrant," to be published with its full quota of tears, and he expressed satisfaction with the general results of "The Borderers." But these evidences of tolerance appeared much later in his life: from 1798 to 1807 he was most ardent about his principles and least tolerant of his mistakes. Nevertheless, in the material of feeling the alterations were not revolutionary, some of the sobering scarcely noticeable. The statistics indicate the limits of the changes in style of stating emotion to which the *Prelude,* the history of his mind, made explicit reference; the changes were all within the stated material of feeling, and the main substance of that material kept its eighteenth-century weight and dignity.

MAJOR WORK: THEORY

In these ten years, during and after the publication of the *Lyrical Ballads,* Wordsworth, in addition to the writing of lyrics, was planning and writing the larger work, *The Recluse,* which included *The Prelude* and *The Excursion,* and which dealt directly with subject matter heretofore simply solidly behind his poetry: the theoretical relation of man, nature, and society. This was, in his own terms, his major work, and it was conceived and executed mainly in this one decade, two major parts of it never finished in all the years of writing that remained.[18] It is significant and convenient enough, then, to look at the three parts that we have as a unit, the first unit after the *Lyrical Ballads,* the unit representing the emotional thought of the poet as it coördinated his own life in his mind and put forth in poetry, where he felt it belonged, the philosophy that was only half said when said in the prose of the prefaces. In such poetic statement the words of emotion were not only necessary accompaniment, not only referents precise and valuable, but also necessary subjects for extended meditative discussion.

---

[18] For the chronology of the parts of this work, see Ernest de Selincourt's edition of the *Prelude,* Introd., esp. pp. xxi ff.

We have seen that in Wordsworth's general prose-expressed philosophy, or atmosphere of terms, there were concentric circles of major importance: one, the fundamental principles and passions alike in all men; a second, the relation of these to nature and natural objects; a third, the special functions of the poet and the poetic mind. We have seen that certain prime topics were for Wordsworth corollary to these: the power of abstract and general terms, such as the words of emotion, unarbitrary and meaningful to all; the power of simplicity in language and life unspoiled by sophisticated subtleties and spices; the close identification of reason, imagination, and abstraction; the emphasis on the universal and enduring. All these are stated and restated in the verse of the *Prelude,* the *Excursion,* and the one book of the *Recluse* which was to have opened the section between.[19] The poetry handles the theory with a sound of assurance, because it does so without argument or much searching of detail.

Mr. de Selincourt has suggested that when the idea for the work came to Wordsworth early in 1798, he wrote the lines which he later used as "Prospectus" for the *Excursion,* the lines which conclude the *Recluse,* Book I,[20] and these lines may offer, then, not only an example of a large amount of the generalizing style, but also one of the earliest examples. This is the sound of the poetry Wordsworth wrote when he contrived "to convey most of the knowledge of which I am possessed. My object is to give pictures of Nature, Man, and Society."[21] This is the "prospectus":

> On Man, on Nature, and on Human Life,
> Musing in solitude, I oft perceive
> Fair trains of imagery before me rise,
> Accompanied by feelings of delight
> Pure, or with no unpleasing sadness mixed;

---

[19] In Wordsworth's plan, the *Recluse,* introduced by the *Prelude* (not named by him), was to have consisted of three parts: for the first of these he wrote the one book now bearing the general title, *The Recluse;* the second is the *Excursion;* the third was not written.

[20] De Selincourt, *op. cit.,* p. xxv.

[21] *Early Letters,* p. 188. To Tobin, March 6, 1798.

And I am conscious of affecting thoughts
And dear remembrances, whose presence soothes
Or elevates the Mind, intent to weigh
The good and evil of our mortal state.

... To these emotions, whencesoe'er they come,
Whether from breath of outward circumstance,
Or from the Soul—an impulse to herself—
I would give utterance in numerous verse.
Of Truth, of Grandeur, Beauty, Love, and Hope,
And melancholy Fear subdued by Faith;
Of blessed consolations in distress;
Of moral strength and intellectual power;
Of joy in widest commonalty spread;
Of the individual Mind that keeps her own
Inviolate retirement, subject there
To Conscience only, and the law supreme
Of that Intelligence which governs all...

... How exquisitely the individual Mind
(And the progressive powers perhaps no less
Of the whole species) to the external World
Is fitted:—and how exquisitely, too—
Theme this but little heard of among men—
The external World is fitted to the Mind;
And the creation (by no lower name
Can it be called) which they with blended might
Accomplish:—this is our high argument.[22]

The trains of imagery, the lists of passions, the elevation of the mind, the balanced phrases, the *the*'s, all come of a skill of expression developed not by the enthusiastic young innovator, but by the century before him. *Exquisitely,* the word which seems perhaps his own, was used by Pope upon this selfsame theme, the relation of beings to the universe.[23] On the other hand, the motion of the blank verse in a realm of sound and sense between heroic couplet and Miltonic blank verse, and the "breath of outward circumstance," the commonalty, and the blending, all are signs of a purpose somewhat shifted in position, requiring, it may be

---

[22] Printed as concluding lines of *Recluse*, I.
[23] *Essay on Man*, on the spider, Epistle I.

surmised, a somewhat more tentative vocabulary. In most of the directly philosophical passages of the work which, as projected, was called *The Recluse,* there is such a combination of the substantial traditional with the shading of difference. We may observe here, for example, a brief passage for each of the traditional interests: the universal feelings of man, the relation of these to nature, their relation in poetry. To trace even in the *Prelude* the varied voicing of these interests in detail would be a study in itself and an illuminating one for poetry; here instances must suffice and for their own sakes draw one further.

Book XIII, in its office as survey rather than narrative, very clearly presents the main outline of the topics in their order: first, the basic frame,

> I had been taught to reverence a Power
> That is the visible quality and shape
> And image of right reason; that matures
> Her processes by steadfast laws; gives birth
> To no impatient or fallacious hopes,
> No heat of passion or excessive zeal,
> No vain conceits; provokes to no quick turns
> Of self-applauding intellect; but trains
> To meekness, and exalts by humble faith;
> Holds up before the mind intoxicate
> With present objects, and the busy dance
> Of things that pass away, a temperate show
> Of objects that endure; and by this course
> Disposes her, when over-fondly set
> On throwing off incumbrances, to seek
> In man, and in the frame of social life,
> Whate'er there is desirable and good
> Of kindred permanence, unchanged in form
> And function, or, through strict vicissitude
> Of life and death, revolving.[24]

This language of generalization in both substance and underlying thought closely resembles the language of such eighteenth-century essays as Pope's on Man. They have in common an ease

---

[24] *Prelude,* XIII, ll. 20–40.

in the indefinite, a strong suggestion of definiteness simply from a reliance upon universal acceptance and recognition of the validity of the abstractions. The busy dance of things that pass away, the temperate show of objects that endure: there is no question which is which, and "dance" and "show" have not the immediacy we should expect in them, because immediacy is not the problem. The "frame of social life" and "kindred permanence" have their own sort of vitality drawn up from a century of emphasized interest. Even more stiffened into acceptable generality is the language of the *Excursion* on the same basic theme:

> Happy is he who lives to understand,
> Not human nature only, but explores
> All natures,—to the end that he may find
> The law that governs each; and where begins
> The union, the partition where, that makes
> Kind and degree, among all visible Beings;
> The constitutions, powers, and faculties,
> Which they inherit,—cannot step beyond,—
> And cannot fall beneath; that do assign
> To every class its station and its office,
> Through all the mighty commonwealth of things
> Up from the creeping plant to sovereign Man.
> Such converse, if directed by a meek,
> Sincere, and humble spirit, teaches love:
> For knowledge is delight; and such delight
> Breeds love: yet, suited as it rather is
> To thought and to the climbing intellect,
> It teaches less to love than to adore;
> If that be not indeed the highest love![25]

It must be remembered that to be concerned with terms is not necessarily to be concerned with the yeas and nays of one ism or another as it arranges the terms. Therefore our concentration is not upon the special variety or source of argument in such a passage, nor its difference from others of Wordsworth's statements, but simply upon the fact of the material of language and texture

---

[25] *Excursion*, IV, ll. 332–350.

of its composition, the sweeping general emphases upon fundamental abstract human and social terms, yet the effect of firm
control and reason rising from the balance and progression of the
phrases and from such terms as human nature, commonwealth,
and the names of the passions. Even the import of these very
names found statement in the *Prelude:* when Wordsworth wrote
in deepest dismay:

> This was the time, when, all things tending fast
> To depravation, speculative schemes
> That promised to abstract the hopes of Man
> Out of his feelings, to be fixed thenceforth
> For ever in a purer element—
> Found ready welcome. Tempting region *that*
> For Zeal to enter and refresh herself,
> Where passions had the privilege to work,
> And never hear the sound of their own names.[26]

A second essential in the discussion of the passions was their
relation to experience of natural objects. Book XIII of the *Prelude*
in due course arrived at setting down, specifically, that relation
as it had been implied throughout the poem and stated in one
fashion or another.

> Also, about this time did I receive
> Convictions still more strong than heretofore,
> Not only that the inner frame is good,
> And graciously composed, but that, no less,
> Nature for all conditions wants not power
> To consecrate, if we have eyes to see,
> The outside of her creatures, and to breathe
> Grandeur upon the very humblest face
> Of human life. I felt that the array
> Of act and circumstance, and visible form,
> Is mainly to the pleasure of the mind
> What passion makes them; that meanwhile the forms
> Of Nature have a passion in themselves,
> That intermingles with those works of man
> To which she summons him;[27]

---

[26] *Prelude*, XI, ll. 223–232.   [27] XIII, ll. 279–293.

All the corollaries of such statements, the theories of imagination, recollection in tranquillity, the eighteenth-century problem of the aesthetic emotion, the simple, the rustic, the power of progress, find likewise place by statement in the major philosophical work,[28] and one sees that for Wordsworth both the history of his own mind and that of Man, Nature, and Society, were involved with the established terms and psychological problems. The prose material of the prefaces, essays, letters, had a persistent importance in the major poem, not merely implied, put forth deviously, assumed as matrix, but also presented and stated in the solidly general vocabulary and structure of the lines themselves. The theory behind the poetry was indeed at times the direct substance of the poetry.

So the tentative definitional lines of "The Borderers" took up, by their vast increase in the later greater poem, the functions of poetic language which had been developing in the century before them; and general statement of emotion as its own vital subject matter became a characteristic of the Wordsworthian style by his own serious choice of material. The great difference was, of course, that the plan of the *Recluse* contained much more complication than theretofore: the complication of Wordsworth's self. From his own extreme sensibility and his consciousness of it there rose a poetry using the language of emotion which, though firmly bound to the old materials, had new bonds of its own. Therefore a great deal of the specific discussion of emotion, particularly in the *Prelude,* is not of general emotion, but of Wordsworth's own: the survey is through one heart's reactions in detail, the generalization follows upon innumerable individual occurrences and crises. The hero in his own person felt too much, did not feel enough, was dead to feeling; each reaction was a major dramatic event. By such particular and singular intensity

---

[28] See, as instances, *Prelude,* II, ll. 376–386; V, ll. 13–50; VI, ll. 584–605; XII, ll. 44–52; XIII, ll. 160–168; XIV, ll. 70–130, 321–348; *Excursion,* IV, ll. 1207 ff.; VII, ll. 999 ff., etc.

the accepted vocabulary of emotion was given life by constant action as well as by eternal verity. And so the shining newness of the face of the larger work comes for us rather from the pronoun "I" than from any major difference in the terms of feeling.

His own relation, as a Poet, to the world, that third major interest of Wordsworth, is stated as explicitly in the *Prelude* as any of the interests. The statements recognize both the individuality and the universality of the material.

> ... and I would give
> While yet we may, as far as words can give,
> Substance and life to what I feel, enshrining,
> Such is my hope, the spirit of the Past
> For future restoration.

> ... 'tis mine
> To speak, what I myself have known and felt;

> ... Of these, said I, shall be my song; of these,
> If future years mature me for the task,
> Will I record the praises, making verse
> Deal boldly with substantial things; in truth
> And sanctity of passion,

> ... Poets, even as Prophets, each with each
> Connected, in a mighty scheme of truth,
> Have each his own peculiar faculty.[29]

MAJOR WORK: PRACTICE

The peculiar faculty of Wordsworth himself, in making poetry again of the terms of feeling as it had been made steadily before him, is most peculiar and most individually exercised in the decade from 1798 to 1807, in the *Prelude* and the lyrics of that time. This long-standing generalization of students, the minute study of vocabulary serves only to support. One might have imagined, I imagined, that the theoretical discussion of phases of feeling in their frame, at which we have just been looking, was the *Prelude*'s great single contribution to the material; that the poetry of later

---

[29] Respectively, XII, ll. 281–285; XIII, ll. 11–12, 232–236, 301–303.

years, though duller in its subjects, as after-reports of the great engagement, would still be vivid in its variations in the treatment of feeling. This, I think now, is not so; presently we shall look at the later poetry. At any rate, to look now at the texture of the *Recluse* as a whole and the lyrics of its time is to see an arrangement, distribution, combination of the familiar terms which is least familiar with respect to the preceding century and most representative of the "peculiar faculty."

In its representation of percentages, table 1 suggests certain facts about this faculty: that in its development since "The Borderers" it had strongly increased general statement of its material, decreased physical location, and decreased to a less degree the device of personification. The total effect, then, was more like that of Pope and the poets of Dodsley's, like Johnson and Goldsmith except for their omission of affections in nature, and even less like the Pre-Romantics than before. On the other hand, in comparison with the immediately preceding and concurrent *Lyrical Ballads,* there was a slight easing of austerity, a few more uses of pictorial device were notable, and in the *Prelude* and *Excursion* the lessening of bestowal of feeling on nature was a motion toward the earlier norm. To this last the single book of the first part of the *Recluse* was an exception: there the affections of nature had an extra importance, replacing abstract statement. On the whole, the proportions of abstract, physical, bestowal, personification, and objectification, in that order, had changed from early work to the "larger work" from 2, 5, 1, 1, 1 to 4, 3, 1, 1, 1, and that was mainly a change in the amount of notable abstraction. The lyrics of the 1801–1807 period, mostly published in 1807,[30] shifted the proportion slightly to 3, 3, 2, 1, 1, which was perhaps a natural lyrical tendency, as in the *Ballads,* toward more association of emotion with nature. It is clear, then, that the varieties of the material of emotion settled in the major

---

[30] For quotations from this material, see section iii.

period into fairly equal parts of abstraction, physical location, and the three exterior devices; that Wordsworth in his increased emphasis upon the first of these had recalled an eighteenth-century power to his own speculative need.

Not only in amount, but also in the caliber of the material, which the chart cannot indicate, abstract statement strengthened. The many direct philosophical discussions, examples of which we have noted, are centers of such fully simple generalization, and are centers also of characteristic adoption of eighteenth-century technique in terms. But there are in addition innumerable briefer phrases, alone in their context, which manage to represent the technique and at the same time to make it sound particularly Wordsworthian. These are some closely traditional phrases: from the *Prelude*, "fits of vulgar joy," "To patriotic and domestic love Analogous," "A never-failing principle of joy And purest passion," "In no disturbance of excessive hope"; from the *Excursion*, "The feeling pleasures of his loneliness," "false unnatural joy," "impulse of a just disdain," "The longing for confirmed tranquillity," and this distinguished characterization from the first book,

> She was a Woman of a steady mind,
> Tender and deep in her excess of love;
> Not speaking much, pleased rather with the joy
> Of her own thoughts: by some especial care
> Her temper had been framed, as if to make
> A Being, who by adding love to peace
> Might live on earth a life of happiness.

On the other hand, some of the phrases though very like these have a special ring, as: from the *Excursion*, "Feelingly sweet is stillness after storm," "inly pleased"; from the *Prelude*, "Fostered alike by beauty and by fear," "an alien sound of melancholy," "by the impressive discipline of fear," "this dark sense Of noble feeling," "And all the sad etcetera of the wrong," "O pleasant exercise of hope and joy!"

Wordsworth's contribution to the technique was, one sees, made up of simplicity and sensitivity. That is, the shading of difference was a shading of delicacy: the words were not so full-blown and self-dependent in some of these characteristically Wordsworthian passages; there was more of sense and feeling, and less of zeal and rage. The vocabulary—*etcetera, pleasant exercise, longing*—is more ordinary than oracular. In such small compass one can see the problems of language that were troubling Wordsworth: his liking of the finely-hinged and unassuming, his practice in the set, matured, and assured. To this latter practice, except when it was too elaborate and bombastic, he did not object; he simply added. The combination of a mature style for the statement of emotion with a personal awareness of the plain, vivid relationship of emotion to sense perception resulted in a poetry the texture of which was somewhat lightened, in comparison to that of the eighteenth century. The "sad etcetera of the wrong" is a good example of the alteration, and of Wordsworth's whole theory; without losing any atmosphere of generality and abstract truth, it at once deflates and enlivens the abstract by the rich, common ring of its phrasing. So, too, plain joy and fear kept on home ground the feet of rapture and terror. To say so is not to draw any fast line; it is not to say that the eighteenth century had not the simplifying knack also, but simply that it was not part of that major fashion. Consequently, when one finds over and over again in Wordsworth that eighteenth-century manner of abstract statement, the list of emotions, one still, every now and then, knows it to be Wordsworth's own by the fine-drawn combination of it,

> Of humble cares and delicate desires,
> Mild interests and gentlest sympathies.

The abstract language of emotion, then, not only more than doubled in the decade of the major work; it also took on a great deal of new richness, both the best of the eighteenth-century emphasis and Wordsworth's own variation upon it. Hearing the sound of the poetry on Man, Nature, and Society and on Wordsworth's own mind, one should not fail to hear the passions' earnest various speaking in their own terms, as these terms had prospered in the ways of an art.

As the plain names took a larger place, the emotions located in the body faded by almost half, but it is significant to see that they did not thereby fade in effectiveness. Wordsworth's most whole-hearted acceptance of his predecessors' language had probably been in this branch of the material; he had preserved through "The Borderers" a host of struggling and bursting hearts as well as some, particularly in "The Borderers," perceptive analyses. The extreme struggles and pangs were no loss to the *Prelude* and its group, because such extremes had grown up out of a slightly different need, a concern for the main lines of power in the body and the major forces of those lines, the gales of the passions. These having become well established, Wordsworth could afford to devote himself to finer and more closely physiological distinctions, and his own physical sensitivity had that tendency. So the traditional vein, though constant, was tempered: "The many feelings that oppressed my heart," "emotions wrought Within the breast," "His mind in a just equipoise of love"; with some exceptions, like "Feverish with weary joints and beating minds," which were still highly effective; and the tradition was used with new weight of detail:

> ...and deep feelings had impressed
> So vividly great objects that they lay
> Upon his mind like substances, whose presence
> Perplexed the bodily sense.

Such lines are, I think, illustrative of a strong Wordsworthian talent for explicit description of feeling, a description where "bodily sense" is present, yet where the whole tone as attitude is general and thoughtful. Another of his talents in the physical strand is for the immediate, the simple, warmly sensed, of the famous "Felt in the blood and felt along the heart" and

> ... when, from excess
> Of happiness, my blood appeared to flow
> For its own pleasure, and I breathed with joy.

These two ways of expression, the theoretical and the immediate—both of course arising from a pattern of theory, but one reflecting a more aloof vantage point than the other—reacted upon each other to this curious result characteristic of Wordsworth and his philosophy: that the mention of physical emotion had usually an effect as of deep thought behind it, that the philosophy was phrased in terms of breath and blood,[31] so that the theoretical bond between mind and sensation was enforced by the constant interplay of words and figures representing them.

Though a sound sense of the technique and its variations can only come from direct attention to the entire material in its context, I suggest the following phrases to indicate the atmosphere: from the *Prelude,* "an aching and a barren sense Of gay confusion," "all my thoughts Were steeped in feeling," "the fear gone by Pressed on me almost like a fear to come," "Whose souls were sick with pain of what would be," "that happy stillness of the mind." Two special mixtures of device concerned with physical location also make clear how closely bound in Wordsworth's thought was the bodily feeling with more complicated structures: these are the elaborately developed mixture with objectification, and the more faintly suggested association with personification. The latter gives to mind and heart a force of their own, as in "a quiet independence of the heart," "the proud workings of the soul," and in variation, "detached internally from academic cares." Such detachment suggests a like usage by Pope, "The soul

---

[31] For an interesting discussion of Wordsworth's effect of logical philosophical argument where there actually is none, using the example of the *Prelude*'s Babe along whose "infant veins are interfused The gravitation and the filial bond Of nature," see Leavis, *Revaluations,* pp. 155–165.

uneasy and confined from home, Rests and expatiates in a life to come," from Epistle I of the *Essay on Man*. It would seem that this figure had a vitality for the century, though it was in a way foreign to the interest in principle and process. The other enrichment from past device, the mingling with conceit, too, is foreign to the major trend, in such lines as abound in Book IV of the *Excursion*, lines 1043–1049:

> ... when the spirit stoops
> To drink with gratitude the crystal stream
> Of unreproved enjoyment; and is pleased
> To muse and be saluted by the air
> Of meek repentance, wafting wall-flower scents
> From out the crumbling ruins of fallen pride
> And chambers of transgression, now forlorn.

Here is a spirit almost completely removed from the usual bodily spirit, placed among metaphors not bound to any direct physical contact. It is therefore as far from the typically Wordsworthian as one will see, except in the conceits of "The Borderers," and its fairly frequent presence in the "larger work," associated in phrase at least with the physical, is significant indication of Wordsworth's tendency toward internal complexity. That tendency after these years did not develop. When, in the same book of the *Excursion*, lines 174–185, he involved the complexity more closely with direct feeling, he had a chance at larger success:

> Oh! no, the innocent Sufferer often sees
> Too clearly; feels too vividly; and longs
> To realize the vision, with intense
> And over-constant yearning;—there—there lies
> The excess, by which the balance is destroyed.
> Too, too contracted are these walls of flesh,
> The vital warmth too cold, these visual orbs,
> Though inconceivably endowed, too dim
> For any passion of the soul that leads
> To ecstasy; and all the crooked paths
> Of time and change disdaining, takes its course
> Along the line of limitless desires.

Again the reminder is of a past technique: Pope's in his *Essay on Man,*[32] lines on the limitations of men. Among these various connections and artifices of physical location, then, the simplest connections with outer objects, with the immediate sense that Wordsworth gave them, are most purely like the style as the *Prelude,* II, lines 170–174, developed it.

> ...oh, then, the calm
> And dead still water lay upon my mind
> Even with a weight of pleasure; and the sky,
> Never before so beautiful, sank down
> Into my heart, and held me like a dream!

Unlike the first two classifications, abstraction and physical location, the others grew neither in amount nor in grace during the major decade. They were patterns upon which Wordsworth had practiced earlier and already settled: the affections of nature as early as "An Evening Walk," the personification in all the young work, the conceits of objectification in "The Borderers." Occasionally all these shone forth in the larger work at their most brilliant, but they had not the effect of intrinsic import combined with personal stress and deftness which the general and the physical had established. The affections of nature when explicitly bestowed, as notably in Book I of the *Recluse,* lines 170–180, suggest the simply stated ties as they were in the *Lyrical Ballads.*

> The sunbeam said, "Be happy." When this vale
> We entered, bright and solemn was the sky
> That faced us with a passionate welcoming,
> And led us to our threshold. Daylight failed
> Insensibly, and round us gently fell
> Composing darkness, with a quiet load
> Of full contentment, in a little shed
> Disturbed, uneasy in itself as seemed,
> And wondering at its new inhabitants.
> It loves us now, this Vale so beautiful
> Begins to love us!

[32] Epistle I.

Such was a smooth and moving way of associating feelings, but it was essentially precedented, while the sensitive bodily reactions which Wordsworth had come to state to the same end were more poetically his own.

Personification likewise was intermittent, and often true to context in its best manner, but not seemingly necessary. The garden of the lady Sorrow, an exceptional instance, already quoted, nevertheless fitted its place, and "hope that laid Her hand upon her object" was a usual type neither particularly natural to the tone nor particularly antagonistic. As always with Wordsworth, there were some almost purely eighteenth-century uses and also some shadings in the direction of his own special style, and these latter have been already mentioned as blended with physical location, the independence of the heart and so on. A further minor variation is the fluttering group of feelings like "airy hopes Dancing," "the little throng of flitting pleasures," not many in number, but with a personified element different from the main tradition.

Objectification, as we have seen, entered into the statement of reaction in this period, drawn from the resources of the "Borderers" technique, however that had been compounded, and increasing a good deal in intrinsic value as somewhat in amount over the earlier uses other than "The Borderers." The device, in other words, was now adapted more or less; adapted less, one feels in this unusual passage from the *Excursion,* III, lines 488–493,

> Stripped as I am of all the golden fruit
> Of self-esteem; and by the cutting blasts
> Of self-reproach familiarly assailed;
> Yet would I not be of such wintry bareness
> But that some leaf of your regard should hang
> Upon my naked branches:—lively thoughts
> Give birth, full often, to unguarded words;
> I grieve that, in your presence, from my tongue
> Too much of frailty hath already dropped;
> But that too much demands still more.

And adapted more, in choice of figure fitted to the motions of emotions as Wordsworth felt them, in one of his most common figures, from the *Prelude,* VI, lines 742–746.

> ... Finally, whate'er
> I saw, or heard, or felt, was but a stream
> That flowed into a kindred stream; a gale,
> Confederate with the current of the soul,
> To speed my voyage;

The same generalizations hold in the main for the *lyrics* of the 1801–1807 period. The abstract statement is a little less distinguished because of the nature of the material used is lyrical rather than discursive. There is perhaps less of that special distinction of the larger work which lay in delicate binding of named object to named physical reaction in emotion; at any rate, the physical is notably often in the eighteenth-century tradition. The stiffening of convention perceptible in the *Excursion* is especially important to the style of the "Happy Warrior" and the "Ode to Duty."[33] There is strong conventional personification; and bestowal on nature, increased in amount, also is fairly used, with some stress upon season half inward, half outward, as "the pleasant season did my heart employ." Some of the most famous and characteristic poems were of this period, as well as some of the most famous and conventional. "My Heart Leaps Up" is one of the briefest lyrics, "The Waggoner" one of the narratives of extremest simplicity and amiability of nature, like "The Thorn," which Wordsworth said he wrote with so much glee; in 1819[34] he was to say of "The Waggoner" that he wrote it "con amore," and as the two poems were much alike, so the two words *glee* and *amore* represented a change effected by the time of the later comment. Above all, the "Ode on the Intimations of Immortality" held in its compass all the varieties of emotional statement

---

[33] If the change in temper represents a personal sorrow or an increasing interest in Kant, still the changed style is not more personal, nor more philosophically current, but simply more conventional.

[34] Note to "The Thorn" and letter, *Letters: Middle Years,* ed. De Selincourt, II:848.

in typical and compact arrangement, even in a few lines presenting the pattern in its variations:

> Ye Blessed Creatures, I have heard the call
> Ye to each other make; I see
> The heavens laugh with you in your jubilee;
> My heart is at your festival,
> My head hath its coronal,
> The fulness of your bliss, I feel—I feel it all.

In sum, then, the material of emotion in the poetry of the major decade settled itself into a pattern that used the elements and amounts of the earlier work, but did so with its own richness and emphasis. And this richness and emphasis consisted especially of firm, thorough abstraction, of sensitive physical reaction, and of the outward devices of bestowal, personification, and conceit. The traditional eighteenth-century phrases for all these were constant, used with integrity and philosophical immediacy, as necessary to purpose and theory of poetics. And in addition, as the purpose and theory were altered by time and Wordsworth's own psychology, every one of the devices took on now and again the particular nature he had for them: the simplicity of naming, quietness and intensity of tone, stress of the touch of object upon heart and heart on thought.[35] Perhaps no single figure is better illustrative than that of the breeze and breath which Wordsworth used over and over,[36] feeling felt like breathing, as from the outer world of air, yet intrinsic to human life. A single passage which governs the eighteenth-century disparates of sight, the list, the earlier conceit, and by these devices, in still simple language, explicitly identifies "thoughts, images, feelings," is that which

---

[35] Wordsworth himself notably suggests his style in a letter to Coleridge (April 19, 1808; *Letters: Middle Years*, I:198), "... if the Poet is to be predominant over the Dramatist,—then let him see if there are no victories in the world of spirit, no changes, no commotions, no revolutions there, no fluxes and refluxes of the thoughts which may be made interesting by modest combination with the stiller actions of the bodily frame, or with the gentler movements and milder appearances of society and social intercourse, or the still more mild and gentle solicitations of irrational and inanimate nature."

[36] Noted also by Helen Darbishire, "Wordsworth's 'Prelude,'" *Nineteenth Century*, Vol. XCIX, and exemplified by such passages as *Prelude*, I, ll. 33–38, 390–414.

follows the definition of Imagination in Book VI of the *Prelude*. It embodies in detail that major Wordsworthian characteristic which can shine in even the single line "A homeless sound of joy was in the sky"; here it must serve to suggest the quality that came through Wordsworth into the relating of things and feelings:

> Black drizzling crags that spake by the way-side
> As if a voice were in them, the sick sight
> And giddy prospect of the raving stream,
> The unfettered clouds and region of the Heavens,
> Tumult and peace, the darkness and the light—
> Were all like workings of one mind, the features
> Of the same face, blossoms upon one tree;
> Characters of the great Apocalypse,
> The types and symbols of Eternity,
> Of first, and last, and midst, and without end.[37]

In such fashion, figures and uses not on the surface natural to Wordsworth's peculiar need of simple statement of emotional relation were bent at center exactly to his need, and one sees, in addition to the meaningful convention on the one hand and the personal invention on the other, a blend and adaptation whereby conventions were singularized.

LATER PRACTICE

This is where the poetry after 1807 went its own way: it stopped singularizing. The amount of statement by the line remained, and the proportions of type on the whole remained, but the statistics do not suggest the "inner falling off," which left the meanings of convention unsupported and uncolored by personal inventions and adaptations. Much has been written about "the later Wordsworth," "the lost leader," the psychology of the mature poet,[38] and the fact that the poetry was inferior has always

---

[37] *Prelude*, VI, ll. 631–640.
[38] For example, see summary by Willard L. Sperry, *Wordsworth's Anti-Climax*, ch. iii. Suggested as causes by various friends and critics are the break with Coleridge, the French Revolution, Annette, Jeffrey, and so on.

been fundamental. I had expected to find perhaps a persisting character in the vocabulary of emotion; but rather than an exception, it is an illustration of the generalizations. Roughly, one must say this: that while Wordsworth's characteristic feeling had the motion of breath, the feeling of this later work had the motionlessness of one too much concerned with literature and life to be conscious of breathing. In the *Prelude* one found the various devices of statement interlinked, conceit with physical, abstract with personified, and so on, a tempering of styles to a unit of stress; in the later poetry, all these fall apart again, taking up the various eighteenth-century channels whence they came, love its seat in the breast, zeal its burning, the vast Pacific its gladness, and Hope its caroling on the cultured plain. The poetic personality which these possessed was vivid and authentic in its own realm of frames, chains, scales, and surveys, but Wordsworth, having felt the breath of a less structured country, was now unable to do such structured personality more than a passive justice. When one speaks of conventions in poetry, one includes the vitality of individual acceptance that gives them duration and drive, but in Wordsworth's later use of the conventions of feeling there was no such vitality, because the acceptance did not reach to the roots of the meanings.

As a value, then, compared either to its models or to its own elder kin, the poetry after 1807 is not satisfactory in terms of those companions. As a fact, it is of course interesting: it contains the solid persistence and the steady stiffening of an inherited and important material. The fact, too, is the foundation of the value. Consider Wordsworth's attitude of mind after 1807. He had formulated his pattern of the world, in both prose and poetry; he was ready to defend by reassertion. His letters make reference to Price, Hartley, Crabbe, White's *Selbourne,* Dryden, Daniel, Dennis, Beattie, Burns, Cowper, Hogg, Scott: he was receiving substantiation along the main lines, rather than shock and surprise from some new horizon. The main lines were those which were already strong in Dennis, whom Wordsworth quotes on passion with approval,[30] the universal passions, poetry's mission to excite and ameliorate them, their relation to the world of experience. What Wordsworth read was what he had already absorbed from habit in childhood and from sensation in youth: it seemed familiar and true to him, and therefore whatever forms the ideas took in poetry which he did not like, he laid to the caprices of his predecessors. He adopted the major themes and vocabulary of a world view without realizing that these were honestly represented in detail by the very poetic excesses he rejected. Being a friend to the general, he was trapped by the particular because he regarded it not as instance but as accident. So the more friendly he grew to the century's inheritance of generalization, the more of its phraseology he swallowed whole, not differentiating between the value to him of major terms and the value of their embodiment in specific landscapes of body and mind which had grown antique by his time. His increasing tolerance of eighteenth-century phraseology was, then, not merely a lapse or an arbitrary contradiction; it was a too uncritical adoption of detail under the aegis of theory, lacking the realization that under the theory the symbols and key signs had definitely begun to change from frame-and-temperature species to breath-and-motion species, and that he himself had helped to effect that change. In his prime of enthusiasm some of the spirit of eighteenth-century thought had nourished Wordsworth in the very inheritance he had; now the letter of that thought came to satisfy him because he was not conscious of its whole atmosphere of meaning.

But also as early as the major decade, Wordsworth had already become conscious of a kind of reaction and an attitude different from that of impulse and rapt absorption; he was describing as

---

[30] *Letters: Middle Years*, II:617, written December, 1814.

natural to aging the very change that was to come in his poetry.
His own psychology in poetic line expressed what has since been
pondered, so that if one gives the less credit to the predicted result,
one must give the more to the poetry of the prediction. The
specific lines are:

> Yet have I thought that we might also speak,
> And not presumptuously, I trust, of Age,
> As of a final *Eminence;* though bare
> In aspect and forbidding, yet a point
> On which 'tis not impossible to sit
> In awful sovereignty; a place of power,
> A throne, that may be likened unto his,
> Who, in some placid day of summer, looks
> Down from a mountain-top,—say one of those
> High peaks, that bound the vale where now we are.
> Faint, and diminished to the gazing eye,
> Forest and field, and hill and dale appear,
> With all the shapes over their surface spread:
> But, while the gross and visible frame of things
> Relinquishes its hold upon the sense,
> Yea almost on the Mind herself, and seems
> All unsubstantialized,—how loud the voice
> Of waters, with invigorated peal
> From the full river in the vale below,
> Ascending! For on that superior height
> Who sits, is disencumbered from the press
> Of near obstructions, and is privileged
> To breathe in solitude, above the host
> Of ever-humming insects, 'mid thin air
> That suits not them. The murmur of the leaves
> Many and idle, visits not his ear:
> This he is freed from, and from thousand notes
> (Not less unceasing, not less vain than these,)
> By which the finer passages of sense
> Are occupied; and the Soul, that would incline
> To listen, is prevented or deterred.
>
> And may it not be hoped, that, placed by age
> In like removal, tranquil though severe,
> We are not so removed for utter loss;
> But for some favour, suited to our need,

> What more than that the severing should confer
> Fresh power to commune with the invisible world,
> And hear the mighty stream of tendency
> Uttering, for elevation of our thought,
> A clear sonorous voice, inaudible
> To the vast multitude; whose doom it is
> To run the giddy round of vain delight,
> Or fret and labour on the Plain below.[40]

To be freed from "the finer passages of sense" was to be freed from Wordsworth's own personal and deepest talent. To observe from the mountain the "fret and labour of the Plain" was to resort to the eighteenth-century survey in terms of universals. The major poetry of Wordsworth intensified each perspective by the other, strengthening Human Love by the murmur of leaves and making the leaves significant by the love, constantly and explicitly. But even in the writing of it Wordsworth willingly looked toward a "removal" by age which would so rob the plain of its murmurs that he could agree to write about its giddy round of vain delight. Even looking back from the period of the *Prelude,* he was aware of a change in his own reactions:

> Distress of mind ensued upon the sight,
> And ardent meditation. Later years
> Brought to such spectacle a milder sadness,
> Feelings of pure commiseration, grief
>
> ... my likings and my loves
> Ran in new channels, leaving old ones dry;
> And hence a blow that, in maturer age,
> Would but have touched the judgment, struck more deep
> Into sensations near the heart:[41]

When the new channels became old again, blows touched the judgment rather than the heart, and the phraseology which satisfied judgment was not all the heart would ask. So, as Wordsworth in his major work looked back upon his early poetry, he looked

[40] *Excursion,* IX, ll. 49–92.
[41] *Prelude,* VII, ll. 392–395; XI, ll. 184–188. For later prose statement see *Letters: Later Years,* III:876, and compare with III:1158.

forward at that which was to come, and one need not be surprised by its coming.

One further element in the later poetry is the addition, explicitly, of a major circle of emphasis enclosing that of human principles: the circle of Heaven. The effect on the vocabulary of emotion is simply a decrease of unadorned terms of feeling and an increase of support by the names of angels, Heaven, and God. God more often feeds the soul, Heaven more often hopes and loves. This tendency has been revealed most clearly by the work of De Selincourt on the original and revised versions of the *Preludes*. His analyses and Miss Darbishire's[42] find the elaboration of feeling by Christian terms to be one of the most fundamental principles of the revision. On the whole, I have troubled little about the differences of revised versions, either for the *Prelude* or for the earlier poems, but have simply taken the final forms; and this simplification is based upon the fact that in the material of feeling the changes have no great import. Some good phrases in the early descriptive poems were removed by shortening, some modifications in "The Female Vagrant" when enlarged to "Guilt and Sorrow," and so forth,[43] and in the *Prelude* the alterations of words participated in the larger alteration of spirit toward religious convention, but no revision was so consistent or so thorough as to make much difference to the material of feeling in its pattern. Nevertheless, some of the single instances in the *Prelude* are illuminating as they parallel the change in Wordsworth's whole pattern by direct choice, away from "the finer passages of sense" toward the mountain peak and thence toward church and God. Lines 234–238 of Book IX read:

> I worshipped then among the depths of things
> As my soul bade me....
> I felt and nothing else

---

[42] *Wordsworth's Prelude, 1805* (Oxford, 1933), Introd., esp. pp. xxxv–xxxviii, and Darbishire, *loc. cit.*

[43] Cf. Oxford ed. *Lyrical Ballads, 1798–1805*, ed. Sampson. Most notable, of course, is the study of the *Prelude* versions, see note 42.

It was revised to:

> Worshipping then among the depths of things
> As piety ordained ...
> I felt, observed, and pondered.

And "feeling of life endless" became typically "faith in life end-less." Most significant are the instances Miss Darbishire points out of "cutting out words that tell of involuntary action in the mind—things happening of themselves, and substituting other words either nugatory or expressly making the mind itself the agent."[14] This was an eighteenth-century treatment of feeling, giving an independence, a faint personification, to mind, heart, and passions; and Wordsworth used it noticeably even in the earliest *Prelude;* his tendency toward increasing such treatment was not only from theory, as De Selincourt indicates, but also from literary practice. Perhaps less from literature, at least earnestly from his own life, came the increased vocabulary of heaven and deity— the Ecclesiastical Sonnets and all the small, scattered, persistent phrases of piety which gave the passions an association beyond that of the human and the natural. This, as Miss Darbishire suggests, was a layer of thought superimposed, and no actual change. The years past forty were not for change, but for settling and an increasingly distant gaze.

In order to offset the untruths that tend to rise from generalization, one may look more closely at this poetry from "The White Doe of Rylstone" in 1807 to "Ode on the Installation of His Royal Highness Prince Albert as Chancellor of the University of Cambridge, July 1847." One notes first that the subject matter is formalized: tours take the place of single remembered scenes; sonnet sequences dignify the single sonnet; long narratives with fairly conventional plot supplant the lyrical ballads. No single one of these poems differs radically from the whole of its period in its use of emotion; no single subject to any degree elaborated led

---

[14] *Nineteenth Century,* Vol. XC.

Wordsworth to abandon his main course. One might expect that there would be a smaller amount of stated emotion in the fixed pieces, but the proportion remained exactly one in five or six lines; the material maintained its importance. About two dozen brief poems lacked terms of emotion entirely, or nearly, except for some border terms, but as most of these were parts of series, as II of "Memorials of a Tour on the Continent," II, VI, XIV, XV, XXIV, XXI, XXXII of "River Duddon," Pt. I, v, and Pt. III, xliii of "Ecclesiastical Sonnets," XI and XX of the "Tour" of 1833, they represented no conscious integral technique of reticence. Here is a poem without statement, published in 1815 (the only title it has is its own first line):

> Hail, Twilight, sovereign of one peaceful hour!
> Not dull art Thou as undiscerning Night;
> But studious only to remove from sight
> Day's mutable distinctions.—Ancient Power!
> Thus did the waters gleam, the mountains lower,
> To the rude Briton, when, in wolf-skin vest
> Here roving wild, he laid him down to rest
> On the bare rock, or through a leafy bower
> Looked ere his eyes were closed. By him was seen
> The self-same Vision which we now behold,
> At thy meek bidding, shadowy Power! brought forth
> These mighty barriers and the gulf between;
> The flood, the stars,—a spectacle as old
> As the beginning of the heavens and earth!

Such a poem is so nearly on the level of Wordsworth's style, seems to avoid words of emotion by such accident, that one is surprised to find so few in the many hundreds of pages like it, and is more surprised to find none like it which rises above the level of the average to the brightness of the characteristic.

Of the brightness of the characteristic there was clearly less as the years went on: that is, of vigorous abstraction, sensitive bodily reaction, simple bestowal on nature, and devices of personification and objectification which complemented, not merely supple-

mented, the rest. But sometimes, even in a poor poem like X of
the "Tour" of 1833, there are still a few sharp statements:

> Are not, in sooth, their Requiem's sacred ties
> Woven out of passion's sharpest agonies,
> Subdued, composed, and formalized by art,
> To fix a wiser sorrow in the heart?

As a whole, the best general statement was of the eighteenth-
century variety, weighted with dignity and balanced.

Physical feeling preserves its Wordsworthian quality as in the
"Vernal Ode" of 1817, "To lie and listen—till o'er-drowsed sense
Sinks, hardly conscious of the influence"; but it takes on, too, some
static forms entirely foreign to Wordsworth before, like the tears
which flood the Ecclesiastical Sonnet II, xxxii. Bestowal on nature, too, is made a little foreign by being a little silly, as in
"Memorials of a Tour," 1820, X,

> ... The wandering Stream
> (Who loves the Cross, yet to the Crescent's gleam
> Unfolds a willing breast) with infant glee
> Slips from his prison walls:

It suggests the tendency of all the modes of statement to be literary, that is, possibly suitable once but now unchecked by immediate suitability.

Perhaps the outward devices of personification and conceit are
best expressive of the nature of the later poetry. They both increase in amount after 1807 (see table 1), personification almost
doubling, yet they increase in usefulness as illustration with the
effect of allusion, rather than as central complexities. Hopes bat-
ten on scorn, there are banners of joy in the soul, but these are not
intrinsic to their respective poems or to the philosophy as a whole,
unless one call it now the philosophy of literary precedent. Actually, in the last two decades one sees the fading of the old power
of the philosophy of humanity in the use of the phrase the "English breast" and its variations, all as local and as limited. In the

last decade, too, the proportions are readjusted in a pattern almost
as unlike the main Wordsworthian as the very earliest poems presented: a lessening of significant generalization in favor of an
increased location in nature; and that bestowal is not a sensed
one, it is typed and exhorted:

> Mountains, and Vales, and Floods, I call on you
> To share the passion of a just disdain.

For the sake of a concluding atmosphere of the terms, the pattern
of feeling of the later poetry in its mild and faintly artificial average, one may look at the River Duddon Sonnet XXVIII, and note
how the bonds between object and feeling are stated:

> I rose while yet the cattle, heat-opprest,
> Crowded together under rustling trees
> Brushed by the current of the water-breeze;
> And for *their* sakes, and love of all that rest,
> On Duddon's margin, in the sheltering nest;
> For all the startled scaly tribes that slink
> Into his coverts, and each fearless link
> Of dancing insects forged upon his breast;
> For these, and hopes and recollections worn
> Close to the vital seat of human clay;
> Glad meetings, tender partings, that upstay
> The drooping mind of absence, by vows sworn
> In his pure presence near the trysting thorn—
> I thanked the Leader of my onward way.

I think by now the texture of such a poem is clear in its relationships; the basic eighteenth-century materials: the list of objects
of sensation and of connected emotions, the traditional phrases,
vital seat and *drooping mind, link* and *breast;* and at the same
time the single poet's peculiar atmosphere: the *water-breeze,* the
modifying phrases of *absence,* the *pure presence,* the *Leader.* The
combination, the woven material as spoken by the single mind,
presents the delicate shading a poetic substance receives by the
very use of it. But, on the other hand, this particular poem presents little of the depth of shading, of the purest deep character

that was possible to Wordsworth in the days when he planned the *Recluse*. Then he took from his inheritance of terms the plain terms and meanings themselves, and less of fixed phrases, and then his own style was central to many phrases as well as some; it was more singular, as it was shared.

POET AND SKILL

Looking back upon the course of the material of feeling, that array of words and ideas necessary to poetry in their time, as they came to Wordsworth and as he found and made them necessary to him, one can see some of the working of the mind and skill in poetry. One sees the several variations of the material of which the young man became progressively aware: first, the set but feeling location in inspired breast and troubled frame of the Augustans; their abstract personifications, and the more vivid pictorial ones of the school of Gray from Milton; then the affections of nature as most of Wordsworth's immediate predecessors in the Pre-Romantic trend had bestowed them on flower and field; then the metaphysical objectification, in its Shakespearean or Popean smoothness as it startled but illuminated the mind; and not till the major work the Augustan power of generalization in its full dexterity and intelligence. One sees from the beginning Wordsworth's own natural sympathy for and skill in this material: his almost immediate tempering of the physical formulae by direct association with the sources of feeling in the outer world, the twilight deepening on the mind; his simplifying of bestowal and his subduing of personification; his sudden enthusiasm for objectification, later turned to a milder establishment of it once in a while in his own controlling setting; his controlling setting growing more and more to be furnished with the plainest names of emotions. One comes to recognize in the poetry of the major decade after his twenty-seventh year the presence of the new elements and talents which were new to the material and intrinsic to Wordsworth: reliance on the simple general words like *love* and *fear* in an extreme simplicity; sensitivity to feeling as it seemed alike in body and mind and outer world; stress upon the figures and phrases which conveyed this sensitivity in terms of motion between outer and inner: breeze and breath, stream and blood, sunshine and warmth, near-silence and near-passivity, season and mood. Feeling was so currently familiar that its names of themselves represented these associations, so that when there came need in the tracing of a mind and of Man, Nature, and Society to set forth theoretical principles and relationships in abstract terms and the structures of logic, Wordsworth could contrive the skill to make the generalizations, by their underlying vitality, sound like extreme sense.

All the while, one is conscious that the poetry's language speaks for the philosophy's concepts and for the established emphases of everyday as everyday was for Wordsworth. The main terms which named eighteenth-century interests, though under them some of the details were changing, remained significant to the early nineteenth century and were amenable to shifts in proportion and arrangement, to individual contexts, as these satisfied either the conversationalist or the poet. Wordsworth's techniques were rooted in his beliefs; he assimilated much before he thought; when he thought about his inheritance of belief in its relation to his experience, his words, too, fell into a sound relation; when his thought had worn a channel which itself was prescribed by the thought, the words too took to the channel thus philosophically acceptable.

The outstanding fact about poetry's language, in this phase in which we have observed it, is its endurance. Like the ideas it speaks for, it is most ready to take on the vigor of an individual context at the very time when it has become an old and imposing convention; it is most flexible under the hand of one to whom it has been as natural in its emphasis as any of the words he has spoken. The outstanding fact about Wordsworth's skill in the use of this material which he accepted from the first is the depth of its personal identity. The tempering, the lightness, the regularity, the motion which came into its texture came from the special meaning the terms had in Wordsworth's experience. When such meaning led him to believe that aging emotion was a more aloof and literary emotion, he was content to let the same terms have their old way without too close a scrutiny. Stated emotion had endured as a main strand of poetic significance for Wordsworth as before him, and the meanings it gave he returned to it in a new degree of particular life.

V. A SMOOTH GRADATION: CONCLUSION

To us, the vocabulary of emotion in Wordsworth is important as poetic substance and as representative of poetic theory. As substance it furnishes in the poetry a constant and emphatic quality which, whether we sense it or recognize it critically, is evidently essential to the character of the poetry and consequently to our understanding. When we are familiar with the vocabulary's consistencies and inconsistencies, when we are aware of its own nature in the poetry, then we are a little more aware of the nature of the poetry. When we observe the poet's gradual learning and pressing of the capabilities of the substance, the material of meaning, then we have some acquaintance with the working of the poet's mind and skill. As to any object made by art, our response is fairly to the presented existence of the work, to the substance of the work in its presented character. In Wordsworth's poetry the vocabulary of emotion is part of that character.

Consistently present in his poetry, the names of emotions evidently seemed to him poetic names, words meaningful and important to his poetry, and through them therefore we may see something of the nature of the poetic to him. The poetic was the significant, and the significant was a set of meanings primary to a way of life, to a world view. In an atmosphere of terms which had gathered within the cosmology of universal frame and scale, within the sociology of fundamental human forces and desires, within a psychology of innate powers and passions or of sensation and association, within an aesthetic of firm general truth or of visual excitement, the terms of emotion had a major place. In Wordsworth's own part of this atmosphere the place was as great. His young fondness for his poetic predecessors, his strong humanitarian leanings and disturbances, his physical sensitivity which eighteenth-century philosophy accounted for and enforced ethically, his growing comfort in the general as the particular seemed less and less immediate—all these ideas and feelings were significant in their universal truth and their simple names. The names, then, had the prime nature and the vitality of meaning which made for poetry. In naming the heart they named what was then the heart's interest. The poetry was rich with the plain accumulated significance of these terms.

We are unwary if we recognize the qualities of the material without considering the values from which they rise. One cannot observe a quality in a poem and then call it unpoetic, unless one assumes an arbitrary standard for the poetic, or unless one labels the context of the term. The "poetic" is whatever a poem manages to be; in any one time, and as a critical term, that is poetry which is called poetry and that is poetic which one seems to find meaningful and suitable to poetry. Such a statement itself reflects certain interests and standards natural to this time and to me. It emphasizes the qualitative presence of art as that represents the values out of which it has been created. It accounts for historical perspective in language as language speaks for men. It accounts for good and bad in terms either of one's own values explicitly or of the context's values explicitly, and assumes the persistence and consequent relative coherence of some standards and their terms. The justification of such an attitude and method of procedure, aside from the primary one that it seems natural to me, is that it can discover in clear detail the fabric of language as the material of art, the material of art as it changes with the changing versions of the important and the real.[1]

---

[1] One has found, too, that Wordsworth himself is not unfriendly toward analysis. He offers a good defense (note to "This Lawn, A Carpet All Alive, 1829," Cambridge ed.): "But the sense must be cultivated through the mind before we can perceive these inexhaustible treasures of Nature, for such they really are, without the least necessary reference to the utility of her productions, or even to the laws whereupon, as we learn by research, they are dependent. Some are of the opinion that the habit of analyzing, decomposing, and anatomising is inevitably unfavorable to the perception of beauty. People are led into this mistake by overlooking the fact that, such processes being to a certain extent within the reach of a limited intellect, we are apt to ascribe to them that insensibility of which they are in truth the effect and not the cause. Admiration and love, to which all knowledge truly vital must tend, are felt by men of real genius in proportion as their discoveries in natural Philosophy are enlarged; and the beauty in form of a plant or an

Consider Wordsworth's poetry, with its vocabulary of emotion, as it has looked in the shifting light of opinion. First of all, his major work, judged by its vigor and coherence in its own established pattern, regained and made authentic in its own style the deft general statement of abstract truth and feeling which had been characteristic of Augustan poetry and which spoke an atmosphere of thought still important to Wordsworth. By this atmosphere and in these terms the poetry was criticized by his contemporaries. They had favor for his emotions stirring throughout nature to a moral purpose. But they doubted the worth of some of the places the emotion stirred through: the idiot's and waggoner's hearts, the smallest flowers, which by Wordsworth's altering of eighteenth-century tradition became surest feelers of emotion because simplest. A grace and delicacy of attachment was for a while foreign to a lingering standard of the forcefully uplifting sublime, but gradually the picture changed from an ascension of value along a scale of lower to higher types of beings, to a potential ascension from lower to higher qualities within *all* being, the passions being the forces for ascension.

While, then, homely ethics expressly linked to homely objects, and feelings rising from scenes, became cherished poetic ingredients for the Georgians, and for their followers today, new devices were already coming to stand for new values in poetry. Objects long associated with feelings became able to suggest the feelings without further statement, the suggestion of a nebulous and far-off meaning became important, and as in some poems of Rossetti, of Morris, of Tennyson, Browning, Housman, a new implied connection of objects to emotion was stressed through a new subjectivism, until at last the Imagists, Hulme, Eastman,

animal is not made less but more apparent as a whole by more accurate insight into its constituent properties and powers." Yet Cleanth Brooks, in his *Modern Poetry and the Tradition*, pp. 5, 6, finds the Wordsworthian idea to be that thoughts and intellect are inimical to emotion and poetry. See also for Wordsworth's attitude the *Letters: Later Years*, ed. De Selincourt, I:274–276, and III:1268–1269. Add II:580, for an interesting contribution to Brooks' discussion of Wordsworth's generalized style.

and many other modern critics call for the object alone, the qualitative presence bearing all within itself the emotional tone. So some of Wordsworth's poetry still survives as poetic in these terms, in the hints of far-off things or the rich object qualities, the latter, poetically enough, to be found even more richly as background material in his prose.

Now also, readers, writers, and critics in our time are concerned with the depth and complexity of the references of poetic language. Some of these find in Wordsworth a value of intellectual self-consciousness to be called poetic; they praise the *Prelude* most of all. Some, on the other hand, distinguish as the core of intellectual activity in poetry its dramatic elements, the conflict, the far-fetching, the root-reaching, the reconciliation of opposites, the recognitions of irony, as these have place, for example, in the "metaphysical" metaphors of the seventeenth century and today. For these critics, Wordsworth's "smooth gradation" is essentially unpoetic; it rejects not only eighteenth-century balances and antitheses which are weak enough dramatically, it rejects all opposition, as by its own view accidental, and moves by its own ideals in a smooth line from primrose to social happiness with an ease[2] fiberless to poetry of present sterner stuff.

One would not wish, from this study, to choose between these poetries: of man, of nature, of far-off things, of vivid sense perception, of gradation so smooth as to be entirely outside certain vigorous English poetic traditions. One would wish, from this study, simply the pleasure of seeing in some detail how the five and more can easily be all one poetry. One would wish the satisfaction of observing that the felt weight of a special vocabulary is distinguishable in bulk and context; that its poet knows what he intends when he uses it; that his intention and his use are part

---

[2] "I look abroad on Nature, I think of the best part of our species, I lean upon my friends, and I meditate upon the Scriptures, especially the Gospel of St. John; and my creed rises up of itself with the ease of an exhalation, yet a fabric of adamant." *Letters: Later Years,* I, 204.

of a fund of intentions and uses which he has directly and indirectly inherited, in language and in poetic language; that his own particular sight and sensitivity can make of the standard stuff an intense and lasting poetic material.

Much more needs to be known, not only of the entire extent of poetic language, but also of just this small part of it with which we have been concerned. Two problems are examples. One is that of the history of the vocabulary of emotion before Wordsworth and since, the classical, French, and Anglo-Saxon heritages, the Elizabethan developments, the detail of treatment by the metaphysical poets for whom words of emotion may well have taken vigorous shapes of conflict, the minor place of the vocabulary today in such still deeply and differently emotional poets as Eliot, Jeffers, Stevens. Another problem rises from the object-feeling relationship: the changing nature of the objects which act, in changing terms, as illustrations, or stimuli, or objective correlatives, or dramatic centers for the feelings; the phases of the world, and their words, as these take on from time to time the weight of a prime significance for poets. Many other such problems must already have suggested themselves if this study has any good in it; for there is lack of plain, workable knowledge in every direction, and the method makes for slow progress and tentative conclusions. In a day when language is a major interest, it cannot be unimportant to supplement knowledge of poetic language as it is thought to be with some reports on poetic language as it is found to be.

TABLES

THE FIRST three tables indicate proportions and variations within the body of stated emotion in the poetry of Wordsworth, of some of his predecessors, and of the range from Shakespeare to Eliot. The fourth table lists Wordsworth's major words apart from context.

The first three tables present two kinds of fact:

1) The amount of naming by number of lines, counting as one every single name, such as *passion, emotion, love, hate, tears, heart.* (See sec. i.)

2) The proportional relations of the main types of context by which these names are directly elaborated. (See sec. i.) *He laughed with delight, Alas! he said in sorrow, the crystal cup of joy,* are contexts of this kind. The proportion of these in the total number ranges from about one-third to three-fourths.

The number of lines used as samples varies with the units selected: from the 500 lines of Armstrong, Johnson, Eliot, to the 5000 of the Dodsley collections which are intended to cover a variety of work, to the 53,000 of Wordsworth's complete work. How widely these varied samples are applicable as representative of author, type, or time, remains to be discovered through further investigation. It will be noted that samples of more than 500 lines from any of Wordsworth's work except earliest or latest are closely representative of the whole.

TABLE 1

NAMED EMOTION IN WORDSWORTH

Poems	Naming per line	Percentages of types of context in amplified third				
		General	Physical	Bestowal	Personification	Objectification
Early..................	700/ 4200–1/6	15	47	13	11	14
Lyrical Ballads..........	760/ 4900–1/7	42	26	20	02	10
Prelude................	1270/ 7600–1/6	45	27	10	05	13
Recluse................	190/ 850–1/5	25	25	32	05	13
Excursion..............	1350/ 6550–1/6	43	33	07	05	12
1801–1807..............	1100/ 6600–1/6	27	27	24	09	13
White Doe.............	300/ 2000–1/6	27	33	20	..	20
1808–1820..............	740/ 7400–1/6	27	24	11	17	21
Memories of Tour.......	190/ 1000–1/5	24	30	24	12	10
River Duddon..........	100/ 500–1/5	30	35	10	15	10
Eccles. Sonnets..........	400/ 2000–1/5	21	14	28	16	21
1823–1837..............	1500/ 7400–1/5	27	33	10	16	14
1838–1847..............	350/ 1800–1/5	15	24	38	15	08
Total work..........	9000/53000–1/6	32	30	15	09	14

To be noted:

a) Except for the first and last items, the earliest and latest work, the proportions are close to those in the total.

b) The earliest and latest items, differing from the rest, lack general statement, emphasize in youth the physical convention of the eighteenth century, in age the bestowal which Wordsworth himself made conventional.

c) The growing literary quality of style is indicated by increase of personification and objectification, not adapted to any changing need.

d) Poems now considered best have largest amount of general statement.

TABLE 2

NAMED EMOTION IN SOME POETRY FROM POPE TO WORDSWORTH

Poets	Naming per line	Percentages of types of context in amplified half to two-thirds				
		General	Physical	Bestowal	Personification	Objectification
Pope						
Essay on Man.........	250/ 1300–1/5	51	15	08	11	15
Armstrong						
Art of Health..........	170/ 515–1/3	21	47	07	14	11
Dodsley						
I, 200 pp.............	840/ 5000–1/6	32	30	07	11	20
Johnson						
Vanity; London.......	95/ 560–1/6	41	27	03	19	10
Goldsmith						
Deserted Village;						
Traveller..............	130/ 870–1/7	49	31	..	11	09
Gray						
Works						
1750–1760 (not translated or posthumous)..	200/ 750–1/4	18	14	16	45	07
Collins						
Works 1742–1747......	400/ 1400–1/4	21	31	07	37	04
Beattie................						
Minstrel..............	300/ 1100–1/4	38	30	11	12	09
Cowper						
Task I, II, III........	370/ 2450–1/7	32	33	21	06	08
Wordsworth						
Works................	9000/53000–1/6	32	30	15	09	14

TABLE 3

NAMED EMOTION: A WIDER RANGE

Poems	Naming per lines	Percentages of types of context in amplified third to three-fourths				
		General	Physical	Bestowal	Personification	Objectification
Shakespeare						
Sonnets.............	490/ 2160–1/4	12	15	10	35	28
Donne						
Songs and Sonnets.....	235/ 1600–1/7	22	22	06	22	28
Pope						
Essay on Man........	250/ 1300–1/5	51	15	08	11	15
Wordsworth						
Works.............	9000/53000–1/6	32	30	15	09	14
Eliot						
Waste Land..........	17/ 430–1/25	50	33	17	..	..
Jeffers						
Solstice............	70/ 1030–1/15	29	50	07	..	14

To be noted:
a) The strong decrease in naming by Eliot and Jeffers.
b) Particularly their decreased use of personification and objectification.
c) Emphasis on personification and objectification by Donne and Shakespeare.
b) Greater likeness of Wordsworth to Pope than to any other, and the apparent position of these together in a line of development.

TABLE 4

CONCORDANCE TABULATION

(Words used 500 times and more)

500	600	700	1000	1100	1200
feel, feeling	die, death	eye	day, -ly	think, -ought	see, sight
hand	earth	nature	heart		live, life
high	heaven	time			love
joy	hope				man
mountain	hear				
old	light				
please, -ure	long (2)				
soul	look				
spirit	mind				
true, -th	power				

These numbers are approximate. The difficulties of Concordance counting are more complex than one might suppose. For example, Mr. Snyder, whose work on "Wordsworth's Favorite Words" is listed in the Bibliography, reaches different sums, perhaps by certain exclusions. I have counted the various tenses and parts of speech of a word as one. Note the large proportion of *feeling* words: 6 of 30.

BIBLIOGRAPHY

THE PURPOSE of this bibliography is to indicate the fields of generalization into which the detailed study of vocabulary widens. The Cambridge Edition has been used as a basis for the study, because of the convenience of the chronological arrangement.

BIBLIOGRAPHY

By Wordsworth

The Poetical Works of William Wordsworth, ed. Ernest Dowden (Aldine Edition; London, 1892–1893). 7 vols.
The Complete Poetical Works of William Wordsworth, ed. A. J. George (Cambridge Edition; Boston, 1904).
Poetical Works of William Wordsworth, ed. Thomas Hutchinson (London, Oxford Univ. Press, 1920).
The Ecclesiastical Sonnets of Wordsworth, ed. Abbie F. Potts (Yale Univ. Press, 1922).
The Prelude, ed. Ernest de Selincourt (Variorum Edition; Oxford, Clarendon Press, 1926; edition of 1805 version with notes, London, Oxford Univ. Press, 1933).
The Lyrical Ballads, 1798–1805, ed. George Sampson (3d ed.; London, 1914).
A Concordance to the Poems of William Wordsworth, ed. Lane Cooper (New York, 1911).
Prose Works of William Wordsworth, ed. A. B. Grosart (London, 1876). 3 vols.
Letters of the Wordsworth Family, ed. William Knight (London, 1907). 3 vols.
Memorials of Coleorten, ed. William Knight (New York, 1887). 2 vols.
The Journal of Dorothy Wordsworth, ed. William Knight (London, 1904).
Early Letters of William and Dorothy Wordsworth, ed. Ernest de Selincourt (Oxford, Clarendon Press, 1935).
The Letters of William and Dorothy Wordsworth: The Middle Years, 1806–1820 (Oxford, Clarendon Press, 1937). 2 vols.
The Letters of William and Dorothy Wordsworth: The Later Years, 1821–1850 (Oxford, Clarendon Press, 1939). 3 vols.
Correspondence of Henry Crabb Robinson with the Wordsworth Circle, ed. Edith Morley (Oxford, Clarendon Press, 1927). 2 vols.
Wordsworth's Literary Criticism, ed. Nowell C. Smith (London, 1905).

About Wordsworth

Arnold, Matthew. "Preface" to *The Poems of William Wordsworth*, 1879, in *Essays in Criticism*, Ser. II (New York and London, 1888).
Bald, R. C., ed. *Literary Friendships in the Age of Wordsworth* (Cambridge Univ. Press, 1932).
Banerjee, Srikumar. *Critical Theories and Poetical Practice in the "Lyrical Ballads"* (London, Williams and Norgate, 1931).
Barstow, Marjorie Latta. *Wordsworth's Theory of Poetic Diction*, Yale Series in English, ed. A. S. Cook, Vol. LVII (Yale Univ. Press, 1917).
Batho, Edith C. *The Later Wordsworth* (Cambridge Univ. Press, 1935).
Beatty, Arthur. *William Wordsworth, His Doctrine and Art in Their Historical Relations*, University of Wisconsin Studies in Language and Literature, No. 24 (2d ed.; Madison, 1927).
Bradley, A. C. "English Poetry and German Philosophy in the Age of Wordsworth," in *A Miscellany* (London, Macmillan, 1929).
Brede, Alexander. "Theories of Poetic Diction," in *Wordsworth and Others*, Papers of the Michigan Academy of Arts and Letters, Vol. XIV (Ann Arbor, 1931).
Broughton, Leslie Nathan. *The Theocritean Element in the Words of William Wordsworth* (Halle, 1920).
Burgum, Edward. "Wordsworth's Reform in Poetic Diction," *College English*, II:207–216.

[175]

Campbell, O. J., and Mueschke, Paul. "Guilt and Sorrow" and "The Borderers," *Modern Philology*, XXIII:293 ff. and 465 ff.

Casson, T. E. "Wordsworth and 'The Spectator,' " *Review of English Studies*, III (1927): 157 ff.

Chapman, J. A. *Papers on Shelley, Wordsworth, and Others* (London, Oxford Univ. Press, 1929).

Cooper, Lane. "A Survey of the Literature on Wordsworth," *Publications of the Modern Language Association*, XXIII (1908):119–127.

—— "Wordsworth's Reading," *Modern Language Notes*, XII:83–89, 110–117.

Darbishire, Helen. "Wordsworth's 'Prelude,' " *The Nineteenth Century and After*, XCIX (1926):718–732.

De Quincey, Thomas. *Literary Reminiscences* (Boston, 1854).

De Selincourt, Ernest. "The Hitherto Unpublished Preface to 'The Borderers,' " *The Nineteenth Century and After*, C (1926):723–741.

Fausset, Hugh I'Anson. *The Lost Leader, A Study of Wordsworth* (London, Cape, 1933).

Garrod, H. W. *Wordsworth* (2d ed.; Oxford, Clarendon Press, 1927).

Grierson, Sir Herbert J. C. *Milton and Wordsworth: Poets and Prophets* (Cambridge Univ. Press, 1937).

Harper, George M. *William Wordsworth, His Life, Works, and Influence* (London, Murray, 1929).

Havens, Raymond D. "Guilt and Sorrow," *Review of English Studies*, III (1927):71 ff.

—— "The 'Descriptive Sketches' and 'The Prelude,' " *English Literary History*, I (1934):122 ff.

Hazlitt, William. "The Spirit of the Age," in *Complete Works*, ed. P. P. Howe (London, Dent, 1932), Vol. XI.

Hutton, R. H. "On Wordsworth's Two Styles," *Transactions of the Wordsworth Society* (1884), No. 6.

Knowlton, E. C. "Wordsworth and Blair," *Philological Quarterly*, VI (1927):277 ff.

Legouis, Emile. *The Early Life of William Wordsworth, 1770–1798*, trans. J. W. Matthews (New York, Dutton, 1921).

—— "Wordsworth," in *Cambridge History of English Literature*, ed. Ward, Waller, Vol. XI (1914), chap. v.

Logan, James V. "Wordsworth and the Pathetic Fallacy," *Modern Language Notes*. LV: 187–191.

Mead, Marian. *Four Studies in Wordsworth* (Menasha, Wis., Banta Publishing Co., 1929).

Moore, John R. "Wordsworth's Debt to Ossian," *Publications of the Modern Language Association*, n.s., XI (1925):362 ff.

More, Paul Elmer. "Wordsworth," in *Shelburne Essays*, Seventh Series (New York, Putnam's, 1910).

Newton, Annabel. *Wordsworth in Early American Criticism* (Chicago, Univ. Chicago Press, 1928).

Pater, Walter. "Wordsworth," in *Appreciations* (London, Macmillan, 1889).

Rader, Melvin M. *Presiding Ideas in Wordsworth's Poetry*, University of Washington Publications in Language and Literature, Vol. 8, No. 2 (1931).

Raleigh, Walter. *Wordsworth* (London, 1903).

Rannie, David Watson. *Wordsworth and His Circle* (New York, Putnam's, 1907).

Read, Herbert. *Wordsworth* (New York, Cape and Smith, 1931).

Rice, Richard, Jr. *Wordsworth's Mind*, Indiana University Studies, Vol. XI, No. 7 (1915). Also, ed. Harold Littledale (London, Frowde, 1905).

Rice, R. A. *Wordsworth Since 1916*, Smith College Studies in Modern Languages, Vol. V, No. 2 (1924).

Shairp, J. C. "Wordsworth," in *Studies in Poetry and Philosophy* (New York, 1872).
Shearer, Edna Ashton. "Wordsworth and Coleridge Marginalia in a Copy of Richard Payne Knight's 'Analytical Inquiry into the Principles of Taste,' " *Huntington Library Quarterly*, I (1937):63 ff.
Shorthouse, J. H. "On the Platonism of Wordsworth," *Transactions of the Wordsworth Society* (July 19, 1881), No. 6 (1884).
Smith, Elsie. *An Estimate of William Wordsworth by his Contemporaries, 1793–1822* (Oxford, Blackwell, 1932).
Sneath, E. Hershey. *Wordsworth, Poet of Nature and Poet of Man* (Boston, 1912).
Snyder, Franklyn Bliss. "Wordsworth's Favorite Words," *Journal of English and Germanic Philology*, XXII (1923):253 ff.
Sperry, Willard L. *Wordsworth's Anti-Climax* (Cambridge, Harvard Univ. Press, 1935).
Stallknecht, N. P. "Wordsworth and Philosophy," *Publications of the Modern Language Association of America*, XLIV (1929):1116 ff.
Stephen, Leslie. "Wordsworth's Ethics," in *Hours in a Library*, Third Series (London, 1879).
Swinburne, A. C. "Wordsworth and Byron," in *Miscellanies* (London, 1886).
Symington, Andrew J. *Wordsworth, A Biographical Sketch* (London, 1881). 2 vols.
Weaver, Bennett. "Wordsworth's Prelude," *Studies in Philology*, Vol. XXI (1934).
Williams, Charles. *The English Poetic Mind* (Oxford, Clarendon Press, 1932).
Wise, Thomas J. *A Bibliography of William Wordsworth* (London, 1916).

ILLUSTRATIVE MATERIAL

Beckford, William. *Vathek* (London, Chapman and Dodd, 1922).
Blair, Hugh. "Critical Dissertation on the Poems of Ossian," in *Ossian's Poems*, trans. by James MacPherson (Glasgow, 1835).
Boswell, James. *Journal of a Tour to the Hebrides* (New York, 1935).
Burke, Edmund. *A Philosophical Inquiry into the Origin of the Ideas of the Sublime and the Beautiful* (1757), (4th ed.; J. Dodsley, London, 1764).
Chalmers, Alexander, ed. *The Works of the English Poets* (London, 1810). 21 vols. VIII. Pomfret; IX. Parnell; XI. Savage, Swift, Lansdowne; XVI. Armstrong, Goldsmith, Johnson, Smart; XVIII. Beattie.
Chesterfield, Philip Dormer Stanhope, Earl of. *Letters to His Son* (London, Oxford Univ. Press, 1929).
Child, F. J. *The English and Scottish Popular Ballads* (Boston, 1882).
Cowley, Abraham. *English Writings*, ed. A. R. Waller (New York, Macmillan).
Cowper, William. *Poems* (London, Oxford Univ. Press, 1926).
Crabbe, George. *Poetical Works*, ed. by His Son (London, 1834), Vol. 2.
Defoe, B. N., ed. *A Compleat English Dictionary* (London, 1737).
[Dodsley] *A Collection of Poems in Six Volumes*, By Several Hands, for J. Dodsley (London, 1758).
Donne, John. *Complete Poetry and Selected Prose*, ed. John Hayward (New York, Random House, 1930).
Durham, Willard H., ed. *Critical Essays of the XVIIIth Century, 1700–1725* (New Haven, Yale Univ. Press, 1915).
Eliot, T. S. *Collected Poems, 1909–1935* (New York, Harcourt, Brace, 1936).
Ffrench, Yvonne. *News from the Past* (New York, Viking, 1934).
Goldsmith, Oliver. *Complete Works* (London, 1867).
Gray, Thomas, and Collins, William. *Poetical Works*, ed. Austin Lane Poole (2d ed., rev.; London, Oxford Univ. Press, 1926).
A Concordance to the English Poems of Thomas Gray, ed. A. S. Cook (Boston, 1908).

Hobbes, Thomas. *Leviathan* (1651) (Oxford, Clarendon Press, 1909).
Hume, David. *A Treatise of Human Nature,* ed. L. A. Selby-Bigge (Oxford, Clarendon Press, 1888). 3 vols.
—— *Philosophical Essays* (Philadelphia, 1817). 2 vols.
Jeffers, Robinson. *Solstice and Other Poems* (New York, Random House, 1935).
Johnson, Samuel. *Lives of the Poets* (as in *The Works of the English Poets,* ed. Alexander Chalmers, London, 1810).
—— *A Dictionary of the English Language* (London, 1755).
Kames, Henry Home, Lord. *Elements of Criticism* (New York, 1830).
Locke, John. *An Essay Concerning Human Understanding* (1670), ed. A. O. Fraser (Oxford, Clarendon Press, 1894). 2 vols.
Percy, Thomas. *Reliques of Ancient English Poetry* (London, 1839). 3 vols.
Pope, Alexander. *Poetical Works,* ed. A. W. Ward (London, Macmillan, 1897).
—— *Works* (London, 1886). 9 vols.
A Concordance to the Works of Alexander Pope, ed. Edwin Abbott (London, 1875).
Shakespeare, William. *Shakespeare's Complete Works* (Cambridge Edition; Boston, Houghton Mifflin).
Southey, Robert. *Commonplace Book,* ed. J. W. Warter (London, 1851).
Spingarn, Joel, ed. *Critical Essays of the Seventeenth Century* (Oxford, Clarendon Press, 1908–1909). 3 vols.
Temple, Sir William. *Works* (London, 1814), Vol. III.

HISTORICAL STUDIES

Allen, Robert J. *Clubs of Augustan London* (Harvard Univ. Press, 1933).
Babbitt, Irving. *Rousseau and Romanticism* (Boston, Houghton Mifflin, 1919).
Beach, Joseph Warren. *The Concept of Nature in Nineteenth Century English Poetry* (New York, Macmillan, 1936).
Blanknagel, J. C., *et al.* "Romanticism, A Symposium," *Publications of the Modern Language Association,* LV:1–60.
Bosker, Aisso. *Literary Criticism in the Age of Johnson* (The Hague, 1930).
Bush, Douglas. *Mythology and the Romantic Tradition in English Poetry,* Harvard Studies in English, Vol. XVIII (Harvard Univ. Press, 1937).
Campbell, Lily Bess. *Shakespeare's Tragic Heroes* (Cambridge Univ. Press, 1930).
Cobban, Alfred. *Edmund Burke and the Revolt against the Eighteenth Century* (London, Allen and Unwyn, 1929).
Colum, Mary. *From These Roots* (New York, Scribner's, 1937).
Cowl, R. P., ed. *The Theory of Poetry in England* (London, Macmillan, 1914).
Crane, R. S. "Suggestions Toward a Genealogy of the 'Man of Feeling,' " *English Literary History,* I (1934):205 ff.
Deane, C. V. *Aspects of Eighteenth Century Nature Poetry* (Oxford, Blackwell, 1935).
Doughty, Oswald. *The English Lyric in the Age of Reason* (London, 1922).
—— "The English Malady of the Eighteenth Century," *Review of English Studies,* II (1926):257 ff.
Draper, John W. *The Funeral Elegy and the Rise of English Romanticism* (New York Univ. Press, 1929).
Duncan, Carson S. *The New Science and English Literature—The Classical Period* (Menasha, Wis., 1913).
Durling, Dwight. *The Georgic Tradition in English Poetry* (Columbia Univ. Press, 1935).
Elton, Oliver. *A Survey of English Literature, 1780–1830* (London, 1912).
Farley, Frank E. *Scandinavian Influences in the English Romantic Movement,* Harvard Studies in Philology and Literature, Vol. IX (Boston, Ginn, 1903).

Green, Clarence C. *Neo-Classic Theory of Tragedy in England During the Eighteenth Century* (Harvard Univ. Press, 1934).

Havens, Raymond D. *The Influence of Milton on English Poetry* (Harvard Univ. Press, 1922).

—— *The Mind of a Poet* (Johns Hopkins Press, 1942).

—— "Changing Taste in the Eighteenth Century. A Study of Dryden's and Dodsley's Miscellanies," *Publications of the Modern Language Association,* XLIV:501–536.

Herford, C. H. *The Age of Wordsworth* (London, 1901).

Hooker, E. N. "The Reviewers and the New Trends in Poetry, 1754–1770," *Modern Language Notes,* LI (1936):207 ff.

Lovejoy, A. D. "On the Discrimination of Romanticism," *Publications of the Modern Language Association,* XXXIX (1924):229 ff.

MacLean, Kenneth. *John Locke, and English Literature of the Eighteenth Century* (Yale Univ. Press, 1936).

Mead, George. *Movements of Thought—The Nineteenth Century,* ed. M. H. Moore (Univ. Chicago Press, 1936).

Monk, Samuel H. *The Sublime* (New York, Modern Language Association of America, 1935).

—— "Anna Seward and the Romantic Poets," *in* Earl Lester Griggs, ed., *Wordsworth and Coleridge* (Princeton Univ. Press, 1939).

Mossner, Ernest Campbell. *Bishop Butler and the Age of Reason* (New York, Macmillan, 1936).

Partridge, Eric. "The 1762 Efflorescence in Poetics," *Studies in Philology,* XXV (1928): 27 ff.

Phelps, William Lyon. *The Beginnings of the English Romantic Movement* (Boston, 1893).

Platt, Joan. "Development of English Colloquial Idiom During the Eighteenth Century," Part II, in *Review of English Studies,* II (1926):189 ff.

Powell, A. E. (Mrs. A. E. P. Dodds). *The Romantic Theory of Poetry* (London, Arnold, 1926).

Quayle, Thomas. *Poetic Diction, A Study of Eighteenth Century Verse* (London, Methuen, 1924).

Robertson, J. G. *Studies in the Genesis of the Romantic Theory in the Eighteenth Century* (Cambridge Univ. Press, 1925).

Saintsbury, George. *History of Criticism* (London, 1900–1904), Vol. II.

Sherwood, Margaret. *Undercurrents of Influence in English Romantic Poetry* (Harvard Univ. Press, 1934).

Sickels, Eleanor. *The Gloomy Egoist* (Columbia Univ. Press, 1932).

Spurgeon, Caroline. *Shakespeare's Imagery and What It Tells Us* (Cambridge Univ. Press, 1935).

Stephen, Leslie. *English Thought in the Eighteenth Century* (London, 1876).

Stevenson, Samuel W. "Romantic Tendencies in Pope," *English Literary History,* I (1934):126 ff.

Symons, Arthur. *The Romantic Movement in English Poetry* (New York, Dutton, 1909).

Tillotson, Geoffrey. *On the Poetry of Pope* (Oxford, Clarendon Press, 1938).

Trowbridge, Hoyt. "Joseph Warton on the Imagination," *Modern Philology,* XXXV (1937):73 ff.

Utter, Robert P., and Needham, G. R. *Pamela's Daughters* (New York, Macmillan, 1936).

Van Doren, Mark. *The Poetry of John Dryden* (New York, Harcourt, Brace, and Howe, 1920).

Wecter, Dixon. "Burke's Theory of Words, Images, Etc.," *Publications of the Modern Language Association,* LV:167 ff.
Yost, Calvin D. *The Poetry of the Gentleman's Magazine* (Philadelphia, Univ. of Penn., 1936).
Zwager, L. H. *The English Philosophical Lyric* (Purmerend, 1931).

CRITICAL STUDIES IN POETRY

Barfield, Owen. *Poetic Diction, A Study in Meaning* (London, Faber and Groyer, 1928).
Bateson, F. W. *English Poetry and the English Language: An Experiment in Literary History* (Oxford, Clarendon Press, 1934).
Blackmur, R. P. *The Double Agent: Essays in Craft and Elucidation* (New York, Arrow Editions, 1935).
—— "T. S. Eliot," *Hound and Horn,* Vol. I (1928), Nos. 3 and 4.
—— *The Expense of Greatness* (New York, Arrow Editions, 1940).
Bodkin, Maud. *Archetypal Patterns in Poetry* (London, Oxford Univ. Press, 1934).
Bosanquet, Bernard. *History of Aesthetic* (2d ed.; London, 1904).
Bréal, Michel. *Semantics: Studies in the Science of Meaning,* trans. H. Cust (London, 1900).
Bridges, Robert. "Poetic Diction in English," in *Collected Essays, Papers* (London, Oxford Univ. Press, 1928).
Brightfield, Myron F. *The Issue in Literary Criticism* (Berkeley, Univ. of California Press, 1932).
Brooks, Cleanth, Jr. "Three Revolutions in Poetry," *Southern Review,* Vol. I (1935–1936), Nos. 1, 2, and 3.
—— *Modern Poetry and the Tradition* (Univ. of North Carolina Press, 1939).
Burke, Kenneth. *Counter-Statement* (New York, Harcourt, Brace, 1931).
—— *The Philosophy of Literary Form* (Louisiana State Univ. Press, 1941).
Caldwell, James R. "An Explorer in Poetic Fields," *Saturday Review of Literature,* VIII (1932):437 ff.
Courthope, William John. *History of English Poetry* (New York, Macmillan, 1895–1910), Vol. VI.
Croce, Benedetto. *Aesthetic as Science of Expression and General Linguistic,* trans. Douglas Ainslie (London, Macmillan, 1909, 1922).
Dallas, E. S. *The Gay Science* (London, 1866).
Damon, S. Foster. *Amy Lowell, A Chronicle* (Boston, Houghton Mifflin, 1935).
Dewey, John. *Art as Experience* (New York, Minton, Balch, 1934).
Eastman, Max. *The Enjoyment of Poetry* (New York, Scribner's, 1922, 1939).
—— *The Literary Mind* (New York, Scribner's, 1932).
Eliot, T. S. *The Use of Poetry and the Use of Criticism,* Norton Lectures, 1932–1933 (Harvard Univ. Press, 1933).
Empson, William. *Seven Types of Ambiguity* (London, Chatto and Windus, 1930).
—— *Some Versions of Pastoral* (London, Chatto and Windus, 1935).
Gayley, Charles M., and Kurtz, Benjamin P. *Methods and Materials of Literary Criticism,* II. Lyric, Epic, and Allied Forms of Poetry (New York, 1920).
Greenough, J. B., and Kittredge, G. L. *Words and Their Ways in English Speech* (New York, Macmillan, 1901).
Groom, Bernard. "Some Kinds of Poetic Diction," in *Essays and Studies,* Vol. XV, ed. Sir Herbert Warren (Oxford, 1929), pp. 139–160.
Housman, A. E. *The Name and Nature of Poetry* (New York, Macmillan, 1933).
Hulme, T. E. *Speculations,* ed. Herbert Read (London, Kegan Paul. 1924).
Jennings, J. G. *Metaphor in Poetry* (London, Blackie and Son, 1915).

Jesperson, Otto. *Mankind, Nations, and Individual from a Linguistic Point of View* (Harvard Univ. Press, 1925).

Ker, W. P. *Form and Style in Poetry*, ed. R. W. Chambers (New York, Macmillan, 1928).

Leavis, F. R. *Revaluation: Tradition and Development in English Poetry* (London, Chatto and Windus, 1936).

Lewis, C. Day. *"A Hope for Poetry"* (Oxford, Blackwell, 1935).

Lowes, John Livingston. *Convention and Revolt in Poetry* (Boston, Houghton Mifflin, 1924).

Mallam, Phosphor. *An Approach to Poetry* (London, Methuen, 1929).

Marsh, George P. *Lectures on the English Language* (New York, 1859).

Matthiessen, F. O. *The Achievement of T. S. Eliot: An Essay on the Nature of Poetry* (Boston, Houghton Mifflin, 1935).

Moore, George, ed. *Anthology of Pure Poetry* (New York, Boni and Liveright, 1925).

Ogden, C. K., and Richards, I. A. *The Meaning of Meaning* (London, 1926).

Pepper, Stephen. *Aesthetic Quality* (New York, Scribner's, 1937).

Pottle, Frederick A. *The Idiom of Poetry* (Cornell Univ. Press, 1941).

Prall, David. *Aesthetic Judgment* (New York, Crowell, 1929).

—— *Aesthetic Analysis* (New York, Crowell, 1936).

Prescott, Frederick Clarke. *The Poetic Mind* (New York, Macmillan, 1922).

Ransom, John Crowe. *The World's Body* (New York, Scribner's, 1938).

—— *The New Criticism* (Norfolk, Conn., New Directions, 1941).

Read, Herbert. *Phases of English Poetry* (London, L. and V. Woolf, 1928).

—— *Form in Modern Poetry* (London, Sheed and Ward, 1932).

Reed, Edward Bliss. *English Lyrical Poetry* (London, Oxford Univ. Press, 1912).

—— *Science and Poetry* (New York, Norton, 1926).

Richards, I. A. *Principles of Literary Criticism* (4th ed.; London, Kegan Paul, 1925).

—— *Practical Criticism* (New York, Harcourt, Brace, 1930).

—— *Coleridge on the Imagination* (London, Kegan Paul, 1934).

—— *The Philosophy of Rhetoric* (London, Oxford Univ. Press, 1936).

—— *Interpretation in Teaching* (New York, Harcourt, Brace, 1938).

Rylands, George. *Words and Poetry* (London, L. and V. Woolf, 1928).

—— "English Poets and the Abstract Word," in *Essays and Studies,* Vol. XVI, ed. H. J. C. Grierson (Oxford, Clarendon Press, 1931).

Sampson, H. F. *The Language of Poetry* (London, Cranton, 1925).

Santayana, George. *The Sense of Beauty* (New York, Scribner's, 1896).

—— *The Genteel Tradition at Bay* (New York, Scribner's, 1931).

Tate, Allen. *Reactionary Essays on Poetry and Ideas* (New York, Scribner's, 1936).

—— *Reason in Madness* (New York, Putnam's, 1941).

—— "Tension in Poetry," *Southern Review,* Vol. IV, No. 1 (Summer, 1938).

Valéry, Paul. "Concerning the 'Cimetière Marin,' " *Southern Review,* Vol. IV, No. 1 (summer, 1938).

Winters, Yvor. *Primitivism and Decadence* (New York, Arrow Editions, 1937).

Woolf, Virginia. *The Common Reader* (New York, Harcourt, Brace, 1925).

Wyld, Henry Cecil. *Some Aspects of the Diction of English Poetry* (Oxford, Blackwell, 1933).

46 ft 85 ft.
524
171 Table 4